THE ROMANCE OF THE WELSH MOUNTAINS

An Anthology of Climbers' Tales
and Walkers' Ways.

Compiled by

Chris Barber

Cover picture (Chris Barber).
Early morning on Crib-y-ddysgl
with Y Wyddfa in the background.

First Published 1986

ISBN 0 9510444 2 7

In memory of John, a climber,
walker and conservationist,
who loved the Welsh mountains.

3, Holywell Road, Abergavenny, Gwent. NP7 5LP.
Tel: Abergavenny 3909.

Printed by Seargeant Brothers Printers Limited,
Unit 9, Pontyfelin Avenue Industrial Estate,
New Inn, Pontypool, Gwent, NP4 0DQ.

CONTENTS

Foreword

Introduction

Snowdon to the Brecon Beacons

Meditations on the Welsh Mountains

Bibliography

Acknowledgements

The armchair mountaineer.

"If you can neither go to the mountains nor have beside you a friend whose mere presence brings them back, there remains another way, a third best only, but often a pleasant and effective way, that is, to read what men have written of them. With your feet before the fire, or safe and snug in bed, you may let those who have been under the enchantment of mountains try to describe to you the nature of their spell."

R.L.G. Irving. The Mountain Way. 1938.

Looking across Llyn Teyrn to Lliwedd.

FOREWORD

For more than two centuries people have been coming to the mountains of Wales, with varying aims, ambitions, and reactions. Always they have found romance, whether in contemplation of wild and rugged scenery or in the more active adventures of hill-walking and rock-climbing. Often they found fun as well. For all of them the Welsh mountains held a special magic, as of a region where, in an increasingly materialistic world, the spirit of romance was held forever enshrined; and this impression gleams and glances in their writings, both serious and light-hearted.

In this book are collected some of those writings. If they reflect, as they must, the changing attitudes of two hundred years — from alpenstocks through clinker nails to direct-aid climbing — they will be found, I think, to show that the mountains and what they have to offer remain unchanged. The summit wind and the stream in the cwm sing as they always did, the hazard and the laughter are there for the finding. Around them still is the old magic, peculiar to this mountain land, which Gerard Manley Hopkins was thinking of when he wrote

> 'Lovely the woods, waters, meadows, cwms, vales,
> All the air things wear that build this world of Wales.'

Showell Styles
Borth-y-Gest
May 1986.

INTRODUCTION

My main aim in compiling this anthology has been to present a picture of those times when the Welsh Mountains were frequented by intrepid walkers and pioneering cragsmen who wrote of their adventures with an enthusiasm and passion that shines boldly through their detailed descriptions of their days in the hills. They were privileged to have the opportunity of being able to make first ascents of the classic routes; clambering up gullys, tip toeing up the slabs or squirming and grunting up cracks and chimneys. Hemp rope was used to give psychological protection, tricounis were worn with pride and alpenstocks were occasionally in evidence. Their equipment was almost pathetic and amusing when compared with the bewildering choice available for present day climbers and walkers.

Equipment, techniques and attitudes may have changed over the passing years but enthusiasm and dedication certainly remains the same, for the mountains and crags still have the same appeal. The mountain game is a religion for many, being a form of compulsive enjoyment which becomes essential to health, happiness and sanity. It may also be said that the Welsh weather has not changed either for the rain and mist have not lost their dampness or the hailstones their sting. However, today there are waterproofs available that really do keep out the wind and the wet. Tweed jackets have been exchanged for Gortex cagoules or down filled duvet jackets, the hemp rope has been banished for ever and there are even plastic boots with vibram soles that are light on the feet and leave no scratches on the rocks.

Whilst working on this book I immersed myself in the world of the pioneers and explored the crags and hills with such men as Archer Thompson, Walter Parry Haskett Smith, George and Ashley Abraham and Geoffrey Winthrop Young the mountaineering poet. I found myself envying them for having such opportunities for pioneering routes in places where no man had moved before in those times when solitude could be found on the Snowdonia summits even on a hot summer day. At the same time one should admire their boldness, when climbing on unknown rock, without the safeguards of present day equipment and techniques, often took them into situations where retreat was impossible and 'up' was the only way. Also, they seemed to have boundless energy, for so often did they complete a hard day on the hills to face up to a twenty mile walk home.

In addition I have walked in my thoughts with Thomas Pennant, George Borrow, A.G. Bradley, Patrick Monkhouse and a host of other writers who have contributed so much to the literature on Welsh mountains. In the end it became a question of what to leave out rather than the reverse.

So I invite you to join me on a literary journey through the mountains of Wales, starting on Y Wyddfa — the summit of Snowdon, once the abode of eagles and claimed to be covered in perpetual snow. It was once fashionable to sleep on this summit in a wooden shack to observe the sunrise, but nothing has changed, for walkers often bivouac there, before starting out on the fourteen peaks traverse of the 3,000 foot summits of Snowdonia.

Traversing the Snowdon horseshoe we descend into the Llanberis Pass and then head up to the summits of Elidir Fawr, Y Garn, Glyder Fawr and Glyder Fach. We are guided and entertained on our way by the descriptive writings of Thomas Pennant, Haskett Smith and John Cliffe to name but a few. On our way we take in such features as Castell y Gwynt the eerily named 'Castle of the Winds' and the strange vibrating Cantilever Stone. On the north side of the Glyders is the beautiful Cwm Idwal where Llyn Idwal shimmers in the sun, yet 'no bird dare fly over it' and above looms the dark and threatening Devil's Kitchen.

From Ogwen, Tryfan is ascended by the North Ridge, passing the Cannon and reaching Adam and Eve, the two summit blocks of granite where the traditional hop from one rock to the other is a unique but nerve testing experience.

Returning to Ogwen we climb steeply up to the summit of Pen yr Oleu Wen and the Carneddau peaks of Daffydd and Llewellyn, named after Welsh princes and we look back across the rock strewn Glyders to Snowdon in the distance.

Heading south we take in Moel Siabod, Moel Hebog and the dramatic skyline of the Moelwyns rising above the slate town of Blaenau Ffestiniog.

A brief visit is made to Yr Eifl (The Rivals) on the Lleyn Peninsula, where the 'antiquarian treasures are of the highest interest' and we then travel south to the Rhinogs, a wild and rocky range where a narrow pass is ascended by the so called 'Roman Steps'.

Arenig Fawr and Arenig Fach are in the true heart of Wales and provide viewpoints of the mountains of North and Central Wales.

On Cader Idris which was once thought to be the highest mountain in Wales you may spend a night on the summit and awaken either mad, dead or spouting beautiful poetry. I have tried it so you can judge the outcome for yourselves!

Then on to Dinas Mawddwy and the high Arans where Aran Fawddwy surprisingly exceeds Cader Idris in Height. Further south we take in the Berwyns, covered in tussocky grass and on the south side we stand in awe below the impressive cataract of Pistyll y Rhaeadr.

Over the large mass of Plynlimon, where five rivers are born, we press on down through wildest Wales across the Elenith Mountains — an 'empty land of green tumbled hills and winding streams'. This vast area of bog and moor has been called the Great Desert of Wales and it is the last breeding ground of the Red Kite. We pass the wide expanse of water of Claerwen to reach Drygarn Fawr the highest peak in the area where two large cairns are prominent landmarks.

From the Elan Valley our journey leads on to Radnor Forest on the border of England and Wales where the names are a blend of English and Welsh and the population is predominately sheep.

Finally we reach the Black Mountains and the Brecon Beacons with their dramatic skyline and the highest peak in South Wales — Pen-y-Fan with its gully seemed north face providing interesting snow climbing in winter conditions. The first ascent of the Central Gully by R. Sandeman accompanied by his faithful friend Alfred Davies in 1939 is given in dramatic step by step detail.

This book is a mixture of time, place and nostalgia and I make no excuse for occasionally wandering into the present time to give a relevant description or anecdote, for I have tried to provide the occasional comparison of attitude and situation for modern times.

There is still romance to be found in the Welsh mountains particularly if you have an appreciation of wild and beautiful places. Solitude can still be obtained away from the more popular crags, summits and tourists tracks. The 'crags rats' of today, bristling with gear and dipping every ten seconds into their chalk bags to push rock climbing standards to seemingly infinite limits are mainly content with steep and overhanging walls of rock. Very rarely do they attain a summit or traverse a ridge, which at one time was virtually compulsory after any climb to complete the experience. But it is all a matter of personal achievement and satisfaction and after all it does mean less folk on the ridges and summits!

Hopefully this book will give as much enjoyment to those who read it as it has given to me during its preparation.

Chris Barber
Llanfoist
May 1986.

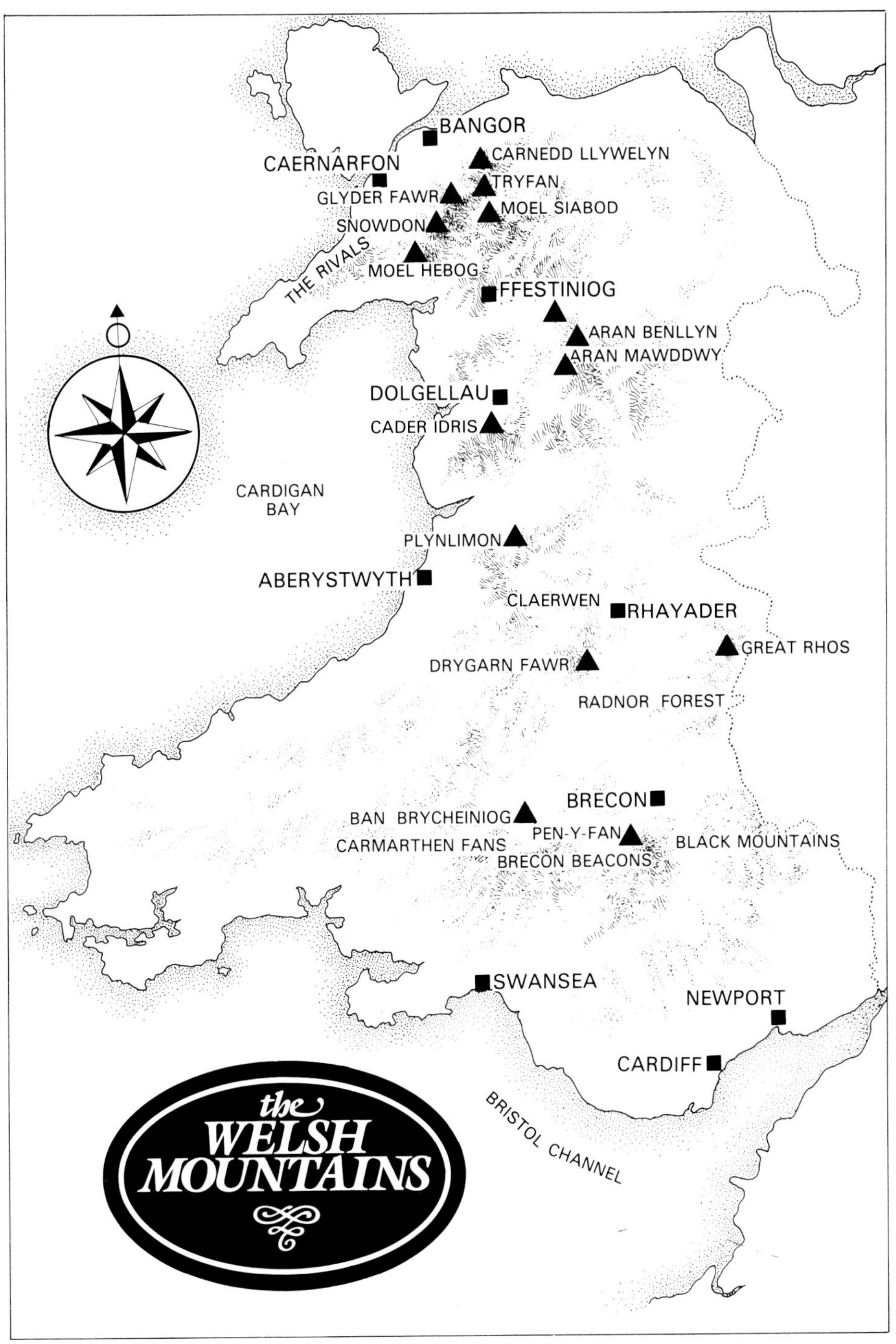
BANGOR
CAERNARFON
CARNEDD LLYWELYN
TRYFAN
GLYDER FAWR
MOEL SIABOD
SNOWDON
THE RIVALS
MOEL HEBOG
FFESTINIOG
ARAN BENLLYN
ARAN MAWDDWY
DOLGELLAU
CADER IDRIS
CARDIGAN BAY
PLYNLIMON
ABERYSTWYTH
CLAERWEN
RHAYADER
GREAT RHOS
DRYGARN FAWR
RADNOR FOREST
BRECON
BAN BRYCHEINIOG
PEN-Y-FAN
CARMARTHEN FANS
BRECON BEACONS
BLACK MOUNTAINS
SWANSEA
NEWPORT
CARDIFF
BRISTOL CHANNEL
the WELSH MOUNTAINS

SNOWDON TO THE BRECON BEACONS

"Snowdon or Eryi, is no single hill, but a mountainous region, the loftiest part of which, called Y Wyddfa, nearly four thousand feet above the level of the sea, is generally considered to be the highest point of Southern Britain. The name Snowdon was bestowed upon this region by the early English on account of the snowy appearance in winter; Eryri by the Britons, because in the old time it abounded with eagles, Eryi in the ancient British language signifying an eyrie or breeding place of eagles.

Snowdon is interesting on various accounts. It is interesting for its picturesque beauty. Perhaps in the whole world there is no region more picturesquely beautiful than Snowdon, a region of mountains, lakes, cataracts, and groves, in which Nature shows herself in her most grand and beautiful forms.

To the Welsh, besides being the hill of the Awen or Muse, it has always been the hill of hills, the loftiest of all mountains, the one whose snow is the coldest, to climb to whose peak is the most difficult of all feats, and the one whose fall will be the most astounding catastrophe of the last day."

Geore Borrow 'Wild Wales', 1854.

"These mountains may not unfitly be termed the British Alps, as being the most vaste of all Britaine, and for their steepnesse and craginesse not unlike those of Italy, all of them towering up into the aire, and round encompassing one farre higher than all the rest, peculiarly called Snowdon-Hill . . . For all the yeare long these lye mantelled over with snow hard crusted together, though otherwise for their height they are open and liable both to the sunne to dissolve them, and the winds to over-sweepe them."

John Speed the Jacobean Map-Maker.

Eyri and the spirit of antiquity.

"Although I am familiar with the alps, and the other mountain ranges of Europe in their wildest and most beautiful recesses, it is with me as it was with Borrow; no hill scenery has reached the peculiar witchery of that around Eryri. It is unique in the scenery of Europe. Grander scenery there is on the continent no doubt — much grander — and scenery more soft and lovely; but none in which grandeur and loveliness meet and mingle in so fascinating a way as in Wales. Moreover to Borrow, as to all lovers of wild Wales, beautiful as its scenery is, it is the romantic associations of that scenery which form so large a portion of its charm. For what race in Europe has a story so poetic, so romantic, so pathetic as the Welsh. Over every inch of the Principality hovers that great spirit who walks the earth, hand in hand with his brother spirit of petry, and throws a radiance over it — the spirit of antiquity.

Now every peak and cliff of Snowdonia and every matchless valley and dale of the land of the Druids is very specially beloved by the spirit of antiquity."

Theodore Watts — Dunton.

"Snowdon (3,560′) is the loftiest peak in this island south of Glasgow, and one of the most beautiful that is to be seen anywhere. The name seems to have originally described a whole district which the Welsh called Craig Eryi (variously rendered 'rock of eagles' and 'rock of snow') The peak itself is called Y Wyddfa (prounounced 'E Withfa'), which is usually translated 'place of presence' or 'of recognition'; but the splendid suppleness of the Welsh language admits of rival renderings, such as 'place of shrubs or trees' which may be compared with the name Gwyddallt — i.e. 'woody cliff'; and even as the non-climber once observed, on seeing a panting form appear at the top on a gully on Clogwyn Garnedd, 'place for a goose.'

Leland speaks of 'the great Withow hille' and says 'all Cregeryi is Forest' and in another place, 'horrible with the sight of bare stones as Cregeryi be'."

W.P. Haskett Smith. 'Climbing in the British Isles' Vol. II 1895.

Snowdon dramatically rising in the background above Llyn Llydaw, as seen from the popular route up Snowdon known as the Miners' Track.

Origin of the name Snowdon.

"The 'hill king' of Cambria, Snowdon is termed by the native Welsh Craig-Eira, which means the 'snowy mountain;' hence the Saxon appellation, Snowdon. Some writers, however, have asserted that Snowdon and the adjacent range of mountains are called Cregiau-yr-Eryri, the 'eagle's cliffs;' but Pennant, whose authority ought to be indisputable, says the former is the correct appellation. Whatever might be the cause in olden time, eagles are never seen soaring over the peaks of Snowdon nowadays; therefore 'snowy mountain' is at all events the more significant title. The highest peak of Snowdon is 3,571 feet in elevation above the sea level, according to Ordnance measurement, and is therefore 779 feet below the level of perpetual snow; so that it is not true — as has been erroneously asserted — that snow may be found in some of its clefts throughout the year. (Snowdon as its name implies is covered with perpetual snow). Nevertheless, even in the middle of summer, the temperature is sometimes low. The thermometer has been observed at 34° just after sunrise, and even in August as low as 48° early in the afternoon. 'In 1850 snow fell here in June;' a phenomenon, we should suppose of rather rare occurrence.

Moel-y-Wyddfa, 'the bald head of the conspicious summit,' is the highest mountain elevation in South Britain; and several eminent topographers, amongst others Pennant and Bingley, have favoured the world with glowing and eloquent descriptions of their ascent to it.

In persuing the accounts given by the older topographers, of the difficulties encountered in the ascent of Snowdon, one cannot help being amused with the air of exaggeration, the inflated terms employed in their descriptions, leading you to almost believe the ascent to be as difficult and as dangerous as if you were ascending one of the Alps in Switzerland. Even the usually accurate Pennant is scarcely free from the charge of exaggeration in recording the 'perils' of the ascent. Far be it from us, however to question the merits of Pennant's narrative; for taking it altogether, it far exceeds in descriptive power any account we have ever perused.

It must be remembered, also, that during the last century and even down to the earlier portion of the present one, the ascent of Snowdon was seldom undertaken by the English Tourist. The 'Saxon in Wales' was rarely seen in those days; Welsh tours were not much in vogue; and few indeed of those individuals who did find their way into North Wales, ventured upon the ascent of Snowdon. We must not, therefore, be much surprised at the timidity exhibited, or the 'nervous horror' which pervaded the minds of those early pioneers who have recorded their experiences of the ascent of Snowdon, or his almost as celebrated neighbour, the 'giant Cader Idris.'

On Easter Sunday, when a seemingly endless stream of walkers follows the Miners' Track on a walk of enchantment with the dramatic cliffs of Lliwedd in the distance.

There are four usual ascents of Snowdon — that is, the routes followed by guides — viz from Llanberis, Beddgelert, Pen-y-Gwryd, and the 'Snowdon Ranger,' on the shores of Llyn Cwellyn. The Capel Curig route is via Pen-y-Gwryd; it is, however, four miles longer. Of these Llanberis enjoys by far the greatest popularity, for two reasons; the first is, that from thence it is indisputably the easiest ascent; and secondly, the exposure is comparatively trifling. These two powerful persuasives will always preserve to Llanberis the largest amount of patronage.

The Llanberis route, however, has this drawback; it is, in our opinion, inferior in sublimity either to Beddgelert or to Pen-y-Gwryd.

In consequence of 'low fares' and 'easy gradients,' a very large majority of tourists and pleasure-seekers ascend from Llanberis, 200 or 300 a day during the height of the season being no unusual amount; and as many have, on one or two occasions, been on the summit of the mountain at the same time. We were told by one of the Beddgelert guides that, a few years ago, a church dignitary preached extempore a very eloquent sermon from Moel-y-Wyddfa, to a numerous congregation, selecting for his text, 'Behold the lamb of God!' What an interesting occasion! What an opportunity for the preacher to dwell upon the 'mighty works' of Him in whose hands

'Are all the corners of the earth:
And the strength of the hills is his also.'

From this it will appear that the romance of the ascent of Snowdon belongs to the past.

The summit of the mountain is absolutely mobbed in the summer and autumn; and such as prefer a quiet journey must seek it in the evening, hold communion with the Queen of Night, view the stars, 'the poetry of heaven,' flickering above the misty peaks, and watch for the effects of early sunrise — 'the solemn splendour of colouring, the chaotic prospect around' — in stillness and solitude.

Within the last two years, two or three of the Llanberis guides have erected some rude huts, called the 'Snowdon Hotel,' on the highest peak adjoining the Ordnance carnedd, or heap of stones, in the centre of which is a tall signal-post, where tea, coffee, ale, porter, spirits and other refreshments can be obtained. Of course you cannot expect these commodities at the usual prices, the labour of conveying them to so great an altitude being taken into consideration. Where such a number of hungry and thirsty visitors are congregated, the demand is great, the prices commensurate; and we have no doubt the guides have found it a good speculation, and reap a rich harvest during the season. You can also 'procure a bed,' if you are desirous of remaining on the mountain all night; but as there is only one bed, in a very small rude apartment, as far as we know, the great majority of the visitors who arrive over or during the night are obliged to 'rough it' in the best way they can. The charge if we recollect rightly, is six shillings and sixpence, for bed and breakfast. The appearance of the huts is unsightly; and the solitudeness of the 'lonely mountain top' — the great charm to us in mountain excursions — is now, in a great measure destroyed. The innovations of man, however cannot alter in this alpine region the external charms of nature. The prospect from Moel y Wyddfa presents the same magnificent combinations — the same majestic views of mountains, valleys, lakes and streams, bounded by the sea, or the faint outlines of the wild Wicklow mountains in the far distant western horizon — until the eye of the observer almost strains itself in the vain attempt to look beyond them.

Before we proceed to give a description of one of our excursions to the summit of Snowdon without a guide, it may be useful to offer a few hints as to the expenses attendant on a guide and ponies from the different stations we have named. The charge for ponies is, we believe, the same at all the inns, viz. five shillings to the summit, if practicable; but if you proceed over the mountains — say, for instance, from Beddgelert to Llanberis — the charge is then doubled. The guides' fees vary. From Beddgelert, the guides charge seven shillings to the summit; if afterwards they proceed with a party to Llanberis or Pen-y-Gwryd, the fee is ten shillings; sometimes when there is a large party, a higher sum is voluntarily paid. A night ascent to Snowdon from Beddgelert is ten shillings, which is moderate enough. The expense of a guide from Pen-y-Gwryd — a much more fatiguing ascent, and nearly the same distance is only four shillings. Llanberis is far in advance on the score of cheapness. When a large party join together, as is almost always the case, the guides' fee for a single individual is a mere trifle. The charge from the Snowdon Ranger is about the same as Beddgelert. From Capel Curig which is a great deal the longest journey, the guides' charge, we believe is ten shillings. The guides are usually provided with some refreshment, either on the route, or at the summit.

Ponies may be ridden from Llanberis or Llyn Cwellyn, to the highest summit of the mountain — these routes being by far the easiest. From Pen-y-Gwryd it is desirable to dismount on reaching Llyn Ffynnon Lâs, as the path from thence becomes rough, steep and very narrow. From Beddgelert the visitor may ride nearly, if not quite, to the top; but many nervous persons proceed on foot after arriving at the narrow ridge called Clawdd-Coch, a part of the route formerly so much dreaded by the tourists. On this subject, Mr. Bingley remarks, 'There is no danger whatever in passing Clawdd-Coch in the daytime, but I must confess that I should by no means like to venture along this track in the night, as many do who have never seen it. If the moon shone very bright, we might it is true escape unhurt; but a dark cloud coming suddenly over would expose us to much danger. Many instances have occurred of persons who, having passed over it in the night were so terrified at seeing it by daylight the next morning, that they have not dared to return the same way, but have gone a very circuitous route by Bettws (Bettws-Gorman, we presume he means). I was informed that one gentleman had been so much alarmed, that he crawled over it back again on his hands and knees.' In reply to this statement, notwithstanding it is backed by the opinion of such a distinguished authority as Bingley, we confidently affirm that, in ordinary summer weather by moonlight or by not, with an experienced guide; and as Beddgelert possesses three most excellent ones, all rejoicing in the name of Jones, the most timid person need not feel in the least alarmed whilst crossing the narrow ridge of Clawdd-Coch. We ourselves have repeatedly seen both ladies and gentlemen leave Beddgelert even so late as nine o'clock, p.m., and when the night afterwards was both dark and cloudy, under the safe conduct of one of these guides. It usually occupies from three and a half hours to reach the summit of Snowdon from Beddgelert at night. In the daytime, the distance, about six miles, is frequently performed in from two and a half to three hours. It would thus appear from the accounts given by Bingley, Warner and others, that the 'terrors' of the ascent have been much magnified; that in reality, there is nothing formidable about the ascent of Snowdon in fine weather; nothing to terrify the most nervous person. Surely the nerves of tourists in former days were of much more fragile materials than modern ones.''

John Henry Cliffe. 'Notes and Recollections of an Angler'. 1860.

NOTE
Y Wyddfa, as the summit of Snowdon was first recorded in a charter granted in 1198 by Llewelyn the Great to the Cistercians of Aberconwy.

The structure of Snowdon.
"To grasp the structure of Snowdon the essential thing to remember is that the mountain has two tops — or rather, that its top is a narrow ridge, half a mile long, slightly curved, and rising to a peak at either end Y Wyddfa (3560′) in the south, Carnedd Ugain (3493′) in the north. The subsidiary ridges of Snowdon radiate from these two ends. (The whole is like the ancient conception of a thunderbolt; a smooth bit in the middle for Zeus to hold it by, and forked lightning coming out of either end. If Snowdon was a thunder-bolt, Zeus would grasp it at Bwlch Glas, where the PIG track joins the tracks from Llanberis and the Snowdon Ranger; the lakes Llydaw and Glaslyn show where his arm would be.)

Snowdon is one of the very few Welsh mountains with a made track on it. Fifteen years ago, one might have gone further; it is one of the few with any track at all on it.''

Patrick Monkhouse. 'On foot in North Wales.' 1934.

The magic of Snowdon.
''Mist or shine, Wales is ever a land of its own. Its mountain walls and shires rise high, higher — and as we think, the eyes are gradually lifted from the nant and its woodlands to the white cataract bursting from Cwm y Llan to Bwlch y Saethau, now stark in the cold evening glow, and to Snowdon itself. The great cone has stripped clear of the mists and clouds, and stands out, gaunt and strong, a magic place, a home for spirits which are neither of this world, nor the next. No wonder it has been the pride of all Wales for centuries untold.''

William T. Palmer 'More odd corners in North Wales.' 1946.

"This mountain the highest and noblest in the district, is bounded on three sides by valleys which in all respects are unsurpassed in geological interest and wild beauty, by any in North Wales. On the north-east lie the bare crags of the narrow pass of Llanberis, on the east the softer beauties of Nant Gwynant, and on the west the long drift — covered slopes of the broad depression that runs from Llyn Cwellyn to Beddgelert. In the midst of these, the mountain rises in a tall peak, 3,571 feet above the sea, its base being formed mostly of old lava beds of telspathic porphyry and the topmost thousand feet chiefly of stratified felespathic tuffs and ashes."

A.C. Ramsey F.R.S., G.S. (1860).

The Halfway House, where tea and other refreshments are still served for the benefit of weary walkers ascending the Llanberis track. This little cabin is 1,780 feet above sea level . . . i.e. half the height of Snowdon, although bear in mind if you have started out from Llanberis, which is at an elevation of 350 feet, you have only ascended 1,430 feet. There is thus another 1,780 feet to go!

Just follow the crowds.
George Borrow ascending Snowdon from Llanberis commented in Wild Wales
"We were far from being the only visitors to the hill this day; groups of people, or single individuals, might be seen going up or descending the peak as far as the eye could reach."

A poor guide.
Hutton failed to ascend Snowdon without a guide for he lost his way . . . "I was a total stranger to the task assigned. I might as well have attempted a miracle.' He later employed a guide but was disappointed for they did not follow a path. ' . . . neither did the guide seem to wish one, less the road should be found by others. The guide I thought inadequate to his office. He made no observations nor spoke but when spoken to . . . he ought to have been master of the prospect."

A hard day on Snowdon.

"I had been from 9 to 12 in ascending this grand eminence; and from 12 to 3 in returning — six hours of the severest labour in my whole life; and perhaps. I am the only man that ever took a wanton trip to the summit of Snowdon at the age of 76. (He then gives some interesting advice). In ascending, if a man falls, it must be upon his hands, which I did several times; if in descending, upon his back, or rather, his right side, which I did once."

Hutton. A Birmingham Historian writing in 1786.

The height of ignorance.

With reference to the height of Snowdon it is interesting to refer to some of the early guide books to the area which sometimes made some amazing claims. One guide book published in 1833 gave the height of Snowdon as 3,759' and the author goes on to remark 'still supposed to be the loftiest hill in Great Britain.' *The author presumably had not heard of Ben Nevis.*

Chris Barber 1986.

Great mountain, except for the summit.

"Snowdon, like the apostle, is all things to all men. It is alternatively an excursion, a stroll, a walk, a scramble, a climb, a struggle for life. You could spend half a lifetime on it, and every day would enrich, rather than exhaust its infinite variety. It is a star with five points, the five great ridges, and five great cwms; and each ridge and each cwm has its own peculiar savour. The only part of the mountain in which one cannot take much interest is the top."

Patrick Monkhouse. 'On foot in North Wales' 1934.

The summit of Snowdon in the mid-nineteenth century, as it would have appeared when George Borrow made his ascent on his journey through 'Wild Wales'.

A dismal place with a good view.
"The summit of Snowdon is a dismal, litter strewn spot, degraded by its popularity and redeemed only by the view. The Snowdon Summit Hotel consists of two wooden huts, where meals or refreshments (alcoholic and otherwise) are obtainable in summer, and where the night may be spent by those who want to see the sunrise."

H.A. Piehler 'Wales for Everyman'. 1938.

The Snowdon summit Hotel consisted of ten bedrooms and two large refreshment rooms each capable of accommodating some seventy to eighty people. The food was prepared initially at one of the Mountain Railway Company's hotels at the foot of the mountain.

Summit of Snowdon.
"The Wyddfa is about thirty feet in diameter and is surrounded on three sides by a low wall. In the middle of it is a rude cabin, in which refreshments are sold, and in which a person resides throughout the year, though there are few or no visitors to the hill's top, except during the middle of summer."
George Borrow 'Wild Wales' 1854.

It was Morris Williams, who worked in the Clogwyn Coch copper mine who first thought up the idea of providing refreshments on the summit of Snowdon. Valentine Davies in his little 'Guide to Snowdon' writes: "He tried first, as an experiment in the open air, offering tea, coffee, bread and butter and cheese, and found a paying demand. The first hut was built in about 1817 or '18, on the property of Hafod-y-Llan, by the Beddgelert guide named Lloyd, who used the stones of the low wall (which used to surround the summit) for the purpose. Later, another hut was built, in competition with the first, on the property of Sir Richard Bulkley, and applications for licences to sell intoxicating liquors were made. One was granted from Caernarfon, and the other from Portmadoc, as the huts were in different 'parishes' (or cantrefs, i.e., hundreds), and so came under different licensing authorities, authorities so far apart although the huts were so close together. The summit of Snowdon is the meeting point of three 'parishes' and of three estates. The curious observer may see a brick wall radiating from the summit towards Beddgelert, and serving no obvious purpose. A brick wall here in a land of rock? Why carry bricks more than 3,000 feet above sea? Merely to mark the boundary of one of the three 'properties' that share Y Wyddfa between them!" (1936).

At the 'hotel' on the summit of Snowdon is a slate plaque with the following words written in Welsh, English, French and Latin — "Wanderer, stop a while and think of the marvellous works of God and of your short passage on earth."

George Borrow — the reluctant Englishman, on the summit of Snowdon.
"Such was the harangue which I uttered on the top of Snowdon; to which Henrietta (his step daughter) listened with affection, three or four English, who stood nigh with grinning scorn, and a Welsh gentleman with considerable interest. The latter coming forward shook me by the hand exclaiming:
'Wyr ti Lydaneg?'
'I am not a Llydanau,' said I; 'I wish I was, or anything but what I am, one of a nation amongst any knowledge save what relates to money-making and over-reaching is looked upon as a disgrace. I am ashamed to say that I am an Englishman."

Boden of Snowdon.
"Been up Snowdon
A nice ascent
William Boden
Burton-on-Trent."
From a visitors' Book in Snowdonia.

Above the clouds.
"It was half past six o'clock ere we stand on the summit of Moel y Wyddfa: it was evening, not a soul was there; we were alone. The mountain during the day, had been visited by a number of people, but all had now departed. We had accomplished the ascent in two hours and thirty minutes from Gorphwysfa.

The view we obtained from this elevated spot was a singular one. Above us the sky was beautifully clear; all below, to about half-way down the mountain, looking towards the Vale of Cwellyn, Anglesea and the whole of the country to the west and south west, was enveloped in a dense mass of white vapour, resembling the ocean billows after a storm. The effect was surprisingly grand, and marvellous beyond conception. You could almost imagine that what you beheld were the raging waters of the foam covered ocean rolling beneath your feet."

John Henry Cliffe 1860. 'Notes of recollections of an Angler' 1860.

A land of lakes and lagoons.
"There we stood enjoying a scene inexpressibly grand. Manifold were the objects which we saw from the brow of Snowdon, but those which filled us with most delight and admiration were numerous lakes and lagoons, which, like sheets of ice or polished silver, lay reflecting the rays of the sun in the deep valleys at his feet."

George Borrow, 'Wild Wales' 1854.

The view from Snowdon in 1860.
"Above and behind us the heavens were of the densest grey; towards the western horizon this was broken by bits of fiery red, which, nearer the sun, brightened to orange and yellow. The mountains of Flintshire were flooded with glory, and later on through the gaps in the ranges, the sunlight was poured in coloured beams, which could be tracked through the air to the places on which their radiance fell. The scene would bear comparison with the splendour of the Alps themselves."

Professor John Tyndall 1860

Hopes for an unobtrusive hotel on Snowdon summit 1898.
"At present the summit Y Wyddfa is occupied by a neat temporary structure. The old, untidy huts have disappeared since the Tram Road Company acquired control of the summit. It is to be hoped that the intention of the Company to substitute an unobtrusive hotel a little way below the actual top where the space is so limited, will before long be carried out. The Portmadoc magistrates were very ill advised in refusing a license for this most obvious improvement on the first application."

'Through Guide to Wales' By Baddeley and Ward 1898.

The summit of Snowdon in 1904.
"We shall probably find the summit crowded, for the average number of persons who ascend daily in summer is about 700, and the number sometimes exceeds 2,000. In the summer letters, telegrams and telephonic messages can be received and dispatched."

'The Gossiping Guide to Wales.' 1904.

Educate the litterbugs!
"Perhaps there will come a time when Snowdon is 'cleaned and tidied up' so that the summit may be left clear and unlittered, and we may be able to regain something of the atmosphere of a mountain shrine, a fit place for lofty thoughts. One of the reforms of our educational methods should be to train children and young people in the lore of the open air, and to help them to acquire a respect for natural beauty so that vandalism shall disappear and we shall treat the beautiful regions of the earth with even greater respect than we sometimes do our Gothic Cathedrals."

Valentine Davies 'A Guide to Snowdon' 1936.

Lliwedd from the summit of Snowdon.

The Snowdon Summit January 1941.
"It was some time since I had last seen Snowdon and I noticed a subtle change. The summit was no longer truncated by a hideous mass of buildings, but stood up as an almost mathematical point. Then I remembered that in response to a public agitation the original hotel had been pulled down and another built at the terminus of the railway, some distance below it. I had taken part in the agitation, and I now looked at the mountain with a feeling of proprietory pride. For once good sense and good taste had triumphed over gross commercialism; though I suspect that the new hotel does better than the old, as the train-borne tourist does not have to brave the few yards between the rail terminus and the summit through mist and rain, and may return to Llanberis happily conscious of having done Snowdon with no more exertion than hopping out of the train into the hotel, having a drink or a meal and hopping back again, which fact if regarded in the right light, is in effect a merciful dispensation of providence."

I ate my sandwiches alone in the lee of the huge cairn, which must weigh at least fifty tons and is a superb example of misplaced energy on the part of those who built it."

Frank Smythe was in a contemplative mood that day and when later sitting alone on the summit on Lliwedd he gave consideration to the possible implications for mountaineers in Wales if Germany was to win the war.

"I allowed myself to dwell on the possibility of a Germanised Wales. There would be fixed ropes to assist the incompetent over Crib Goch, pitons desecrating the crags of Lliwedd, a raucous beer-garden on the top of Snowdon, together with hordes of fat Teutons and their stodgy Fraus. My experience of Germans had convinced me that they do not love Nature in the selfless manner of the Englishman, as in the case of their 'New Order', they like a Nature that can be adapted to their needs, tamed and subservient. Then they can lavish sentiment on it: on the forests with their well made paths, belvederes and beer gardens; on the waterfall that meekly descends over its concreted drop; on the mountain that is shackled in ropes, steps and ladders. And when Nature refuses to be tamed, when Himalayan giants disdain their would-be conquerors, when plans and methods go by the board, the Teuton is hurt, angry and amazed. That any German should be so treated! Then he returns, waving his flags, full of patriotic zeal, determined to overcome and subdue the enemy."

F.S. Smythe 'The Mountain Vision' 1941.

Just for the record.
In September 1923 the Hon. Victor Bruce drove his six cylinder, 16 h.p. car to the summit of Snowdon in two hours and five minutes. He then came down again in one hour forty five minutes. However he was not the first person to undertake this automobile ascent for it was previously done in 1903 by Sir William Letts who drove to the summit in a 7 h.p. light car in less than one hour.

In 1933 the Archbishop of York (Dr. William Temple) recorded that his father climbed Snowdon six times in five days. He described how his father "was staying in that region and thought that the walk over the top was the best in the neighbourhood, from Llanberis to Beddgelert one day and back the next; this he did on five days, but on the fifth he remembered that he had that day bought a bottle of ginger-beer at the top where there was only a little shelter, and had not paid for it, so he walked up again after tea to deposit his sixpence!"

On one day in August 1898, two thousand two hundred people are said to have ascended to the summit.

"To Snowdon's top we came I wist
  Both wet and hungry too
Wherefore so dense we view'd the mist
  And quite we missed the view."

Anon.

A Countryside Commission Census in 1977 revealed that some 400,000 visitors ascend to the summit each year.

Snowdon in reverse.
In May 1981 Len Chivers of Cross Keys, Gwent walked up Snowdon from Pen-y-Pass backwards. He was accompanied by his wife Ann and son Michael and he found it 'much easier' than he had expected it to be. The walk took him 3½ hours and he raised a sum of money for the Jane Hodge Home for Handicapped children at Cowbridge in West Glamorgan. The following day he commenced walking home to Cross Keys in Gwent — walking in a forward direction.

Lliwedd from the summit of Snowdon

A night ascent of Snowdon via the Llanberis path.
"One Saturday night, after a brief restless sleep, I rose at 12.40 and looked out at the pale stars on a night in May. The body said 'Get back to bed.' I did. Presently a clock struck 'one,' and the spirit moved! After due preparation, a start was made at 1.40 a.m., the body protesting that sleep had been insufficient, and the feet stumbling in the darkness. How weird the silent village! How dark the whole, save there, where a lighted bedroom window tells of sickness, or the coming of a child into the world. Through the wood I plod; a loud sigh from under a tree surprises me. It is from a piebald cow and nothing more! The waterfall is not asleep, it sounds more important and persistent now that the normal sounds of day have died away. Some loose slate clatters downwards on the quarry tips; a cuckoo calls.

On, and upwards, the exertion producing warmth and perspiration. Familiar mountain forms seem unfamiliar in the faint light, their dim outlines and slopes take on new forms and steepness. A sheep jumps up startled, and startling. A haze hangs over the lake, the sound of water is borne on a fitful breeze.

On and up! A bird whistles, a cuckoo calls. A streak of light in the sky over the shoulder of Elidyr, faint yet, coming from the north-east shows that it is a herald of the sun. I push on and presently I look down into the Pass, into a deserted land. The Glyders seem terrible, I am alone in an empty world.

I must go on, and up. I walk silently on the springy turf, breathing deeply and quietly, because 'all heaven and earth are still,' and I sense something of the Creator's preparation for a new day.

Shall I be in time? Push on, and increase speed a little. Below, on the right, Llyn Du'r Arddu is a sheet of polished steel. Light is increasing and the track is visible; jutting rocks are seen and avoided. Two sheep jump up, whistling in alarm. A glow tinges the north-eastern sky above the Glyders. A haze falls on the valleys, the mountains behind are dim and shadowy. A final spurt — the summit; a cool breeze; ascend the cairn and sit facing the east-north-east.

The air is chilling; rocks are wet with dew, one's breath makes little clouds as one sits quietly on the cairn. But see! the haze to the north-east suddenly shows a red spot; the spot enlarges, becomes a burning hemisphere, and grows to a flaming disc- the sun! Yes, the glorious sun, unheralded and without sounding of trumpets.

The sun has pierced the curtain of night, a new day has come — a Whit-sun day — and all that it holds in store for the millions in the valleys and plains below me. I am alone, the only watcher of this glorious advent."

Valentine Davies 'A Guide to Snowdon' 1936.

The causeway across Llyn Llydaw with the Summit of Crib Goch towering above.

On the Miners' Track beside Llyn Llydaw with Lliwedd in the background.

Cwm Dyli (pronounced Dully) "is the great eastern recess of Snowdon, and universally admitted to be the finest thing of the kind in Wales. The long sharp ridge of Grib Goch and Grib y Ddysgl bounds it on the north, while the almost equally fine, though less regular ridge and majestic crags of Lliwed shut it on the south. It contains Llyn Llydaw, the largest lake and Glaslyn the finest tarn on the whole mountain, and is one reason why the ascent of Snowdon from Capel Curig is the finest of all."

'Cwm Dyli was the scene in 1875 of one of the strangest of all the disasters which have happened on the mountain. (Snowdon). The victim was Mr. Edward Grindley Kendal, of Crosby, near Leicester, who on June 11, left Cynnant Valley in order to ascend Snowdon. Nothing more was heard of him until the end of that month, when a Mr. and Mrs. David Moseley, descending with a guide, found on the edge of Llyn Llydaw a wet and mouldy pair of boots, each containing a stocking marked 'Kendal' and a garter. It was at once surmised that the missing man had been wading and become engulphed in quicksands, which were stated to be numerous.

His friends went so far as to employ a professional diver to explore the bottom of the lake, though it would seem that if the body was in the water simpler means would have answered the purpose, and if it was below the water the diver could neither find it nor follow it. At any rate he did not find it because it was not there. It was found about ten days later on Crib-y-Ddysgl uninjured — it was identified by Mr. Ison, brother-in-law of the deceased — and the jury at Llanberis found a verdict of 'death by exposure'. It was not precisely stated on what part of Crib-y-Ddysgyl the body was found, and nothing transpired as to the condition of the feet; but it is simply amazing to anyone familiar with the character of the ground that a bare-footed man should ever have got so far. Why he did it and how he did it will always remain among the great mysteries of Snowdon."

W.P. Haskett Smith. 'Climbing in the British Isles'. Vol. II 1895.

Snowdon and Glaslyn. Photo — George and Ashley Abraham.

What they need is glas's.

"It may be mentioned that many people get hopelessly confused in reading or giving descriptions of Snowdon, because they fail to distinguish Glaslyn here from Llyn Glas, half a mile to the north of it, in Cwm Glas, and another Llyn Glas less than a mile due west in Cwm Clogwyn. If they know Glaslyn they naturally assume that it must be in Cwm Glas, and if they know Cwm Glas they place Glaslyn in it. Some of the confusion would be avoided if the latter were called by what would seem to be its older and truer name — Llynffyn nonglas."

W.P. Haskett Smith. 'Climbing in the British Isles'. Vol. II 1895.

Clogwyn y Garnedd y Wyddfa.

(Precipice under the Cairn of Snowdon).

"For more than two centuries this precipice has been famous as a refuge for rare ferns and plants. The guide William Williams, well known as a botanist, lost his life here while in search of the Woodsia; so at least says Mr. T.G. Bonney, though he is far from accurate in the date of the accident, which, writing in 1874, he describes as having taken place 'some twenty years ago.' The actual date was June 19, 1861. The old guide had taken up a lady and gentleman from Llanberis, and went from the top alone to gather ferns. The fall was 'down a declevity of three hundred yards'. The body was found at the foot of the precipice after 'scouts' had been sent out. He had fallen from the point where the slope suddenly changes from about 45° to perhaps, 75° or 80°. The spot where he slipped was for many years, and perhaps still is, marked by a white stone."

W.P. Haskett Smith. 'Climbing in the British Isles' Vol. II 1895.

"The rocks of this face are for the most part dangerously loose and such climbs as there are lie up the gullies seeming it. These are liable to be both difficult and dangerous, difficult because of unusual obstacles jettisoned from the summit hotel, which are said to range from broken-

down bedsteads and perambulators to discarded corsets belts and dangerous because of tourists who engage in the fascinating pursuit of hurling down stones from the summit."
F.S. Smyth 'Over Welsh Hills'. 1945.

Clogwyn du'Arddu — 'the black cliff of the black height' — generally referred to as 'Cloggy' by most climbers with varying degrees of awe and affection. Photo — George & Ashley Abraham.

The hard men of the 1920's.'
"Many of the pioneering climbers of this generation were keen motorists . . . trained in this school of fast driving and hard climbing was Jack Longland, who became one of the great Cambridge leaders. With his scientific technique, Jack Longland was the first to complete a route up the West Buttress of Clogwyn d'ur Arddu. This was a great event, representing a combined effort of Longland and Piggot, with Morley Wood, W. Eversoles and Frank Smythe following."

Kretschmer.

Bivouackers may be interested in visiting a large rock known as Maen D'ur Arddu (said to weigh 5,000 tons) situated on the flanks of Snowdon, near Llyn Du' Arddu. Here the Cader Idris summit legend is repeated. If a man sleeps on this rock for a night, he will awake in the morning either a raving madman or a brilliant poet. *(see page 91).*

A break from the rain.
"An old Welshman was once met by a tourist after a week of persistent rain and asked if it ever did anything but rain in the mountains of Snowdonia. 'Yes he answered, — 'it sometimes snows!' "

Anon.

The Snowdon Horseshoe.

Generally regarded as one of the finest ridge walks in Britain this route was pioneered by C.A.O. Baumgartner who was described as a 'powerfully built fell walker'. In 1847 he made the first recorded traverse of the Crib Goch arête and then carried on over the summits of Snowdon and Lliwedd.

Above Bwlch y Saethau — 'The Pass of the Arrows' — between Snowdon and Lliwedd (in the background). This was one of the legendary locations where King Arthur is supposed to have fought his last battle.

For more detailed history of the route we shall now turn to the writings of W.P. Haskett Smith.

"Any mountaineer worthy of the name will admit that the ridge walk up Snowdon by Lliwedd and down by Grib Goch is for its length one of the finest in Europe. The mere gymnast also finds here plenty of enjoyment and almost infinite variety. He may mount by the east ridge or by the north ridge, or in the corner between the two.

Thirty years ago this ridge was almost unknown. A writer of 1833 seems to imply that it had been ascended by saying that 'the passage of it is hazardous, from the shortness and slippery quality of the grass at those seasons of the year when the mountain may be approached;' but this is evidently a misapplication of what others had said about Clawdd Goch (Bwlch y Maen) on the other side of the mountain, and we do not hear of anyone climbing here before C.A.O.B. (1847) and F.H.B. a few years later. Between 1865 and 1875 it became better known and in the books at Pen-y-Gwryd we find it recorded that in April 1884 H. and C.S. climbed from Cwm Dyli, thence along the ridge by Crib y Ddysgl to the summit of Y Wyddfa.

In 1887, on June 30, E.K. climbed Grib Goch from Cwm Glas by the gully to the left of the outstanding or Crazy Pinnacle. Near the top two big stones are jammed in, and this compelled him to leave the gully; but on June 29, 1890, G.S.S. found these stones climable by the aid of a crack in the rocks on the far left hand. From this point the ridge can be reached by taking to the rocks on the right. They are sound, which is more than can be said for those on the left of the gully a little further down.'
Crib y Ddysgl (Old name Carnedd Ugain).
'The name is pronounced practically 'Cribbythiskle' and sometimes written 'Distyl,' a spelling probably due to a desire to support the common derivation of the name from 'destillane' — i.e. 'dripping ridge'. The climate of Wales, however is not such as to make any ridge remarkable merely because it drips . . .'

The highest point of C.y.D. is called Carnedd Ugain, and is a worthy rival of Y Wyddfa itself, being according to the Ordnance surveyors, only 69′ lower — viz. 3,491′ — and from some points of view a really beautiful peak.

The ridge, though sharp, is not a likely place for an accident to a climber and indeed, no accident seems to have occurred actually on the ridge, but more than one death has taken place close by. On August 10, 1874, a young man of great promise, Mr. Frederick Roberts Wilton, son of Mr. Robert Wilton, of Doncaster, and a master in the City of London School, ascended Snowdon from Llanberis and seems to have asked his way to Capel Curig, and to have been informed (not quite accurately) that he must turn to the right 'near the spring', which is a good bit beyond the proper place of divergence from the Llanberis path. His body was ultimately found a fortnight later in the slippery course of a small mountain stream which descends sharply from the most southerly branch of the miners' path immediately below Crib y Ddysgl into the basin known as Cwm Glas. Evidently he had gone down a steep shingly slope with a wall of rock on his right hand over the entrance of a rocky watercourse'.

These details were taken from a letter of his colleague, Mr. W.G. Rushbrooke. As the body was found in a posture of repose, and there was no sign of any injury sufficient to cause death, there is some reason to fear that this unfortunate gentleman died of exposure. For further details see the Times for August 22, 24, 26 and 28, 1874."

Unfathomable abysses on either side!
"The circuit of the 'Horseshoe of Snowdon' may be described as the finest mountain walk in Britain. The narrow ridge of Grib Goch leading thence to the Pinnacles is unique on British mountains. An average tourist has described it as a 'pointed ridge of rock a mile long, as thin and unsteady as a tightrope, with unfathomable abysses on either side gleaming with the bleached bones of my predecessors'.

The latter probably refers to the remains of some mountain sheep, for no fatal accident had then occurred on Grib Goch.

It is no uncommon site in the summer-time to see some unhappy tourist doing 'a stomach traverse' along the south side of the ridge with his heart in his mouth and perchance something worse.''

George D. Abraham 'British Mountain Climbs' 1909.

A typical summer day on Crib Goch. With few passing places, progress is often frustratingly at a snail's pace, particularly if someone ahead has an attack of nerves or vetigo.

Crib Goch — a wicked ridge, as straight as a rat's tail.
''The pass of Llanberis, 2,500′ below, is a faint unreal link with the life of man. But what impressed me more than anything else, I think, was the north ridge of Grib Goch, a wicked ridge, straight as a rat's tail, plunging downwards to end in the great crag of Dinas Mot, and flanked by rusty-red sullen screes.

The next half mile or so is along the actual crest. The cautious walk with their feet just below the top, on the south side, and use the highest rocks as a handrail. The exuberant walk more or less along the top, waving their arms in the air to show how well they balance. Those whose nerves have failed them have been known to sit astride the ridge and so to crawl painfully along it.''

Patrick Monkhouse 'On foot in North Wales'. 1934.

Crib Goch (the Red Ridge). ''Some have thought it sensational, and many have described its terrors in very sensational language; in fact it takes the place which among the English Lakes is filled by the far less striking Striding Edge on Helvellyn; but in truth, though it is the sort of place where ice, mist, and high wind may encroach to some extent on the margin of safety, to a steady hand and foot there is no danger whatsoever. As for the hands, they are hardly required at all, though for those who like it plenty of real climbing can be had on the way.''

W.P. Haskett Smith 'Climbing in the British Isles' Vol II 1895.

Snowdon from the Pinnacles of Crib Goch — George and Ashley Abraham.

A Winter traverse of the Snowdon Horseshoe.
''This famous mountain walk, with the few hundred feet of easy scrambling that it involves is one of the grandest in Britain, with its quarternion of peaks, its magnificent precipices and the views.

Our announcement in the coffee room (at Pen-y-Pass) that we meant to do the horseshoe as a first day's excursion with a lady in the party too, had provoked comment. Were these some of those mad fell-walkers from the Lakes, who think little of devouring 50 miles and a dozen summits in 24 hours? Our conduct was not reprehensible.

The crest is a knife-edge having on one side the wall of Cwm Glas and the precipitious slope into Cwm Dyli on the other. Puffs of wind now and then shook up the general density, giving transient glimpses of the snows and rocks far below in Cwm Glas; on the other side all continued blank. We wriggled along the narrower parts, sometimes astride; we crawled and clambered and balanced upright along the sharp edge, making the most of every sporting bit; and where the ridge split into a cluster of shivered blocks, two went down the broken end and out to the Crazy Pinnacle itself, up one side and down the other, in spite of the wet and slippery state of the rock and of the wind blowing wildly up the contiguous gully. The other party left us at Bwlch Goch, the gap beyond the Crib, to go off on some secret enterprise of their own, and we five went forward up the rocks of Crib-y-Ddysgl on the abrupt extremity of this higher ridge, the two who were suffering most from that fell disease Cacoethes Scandeni, or climber's evil, found a pair of vertical chimneys that clearly offered the most indirect and impracticable way up the cliff, and refreshed their muscles with a little unnecessary exertion.'

All the way along the ridge we went blindfold so far as the views were concerned. Snow lay in thick drifts around Snowdon summit, and the line was blocked, although we heard that a train had been run to a considerable altitude on the previous day. With the wooden erections all shut up, the spot looked like the forsaken depot of an exploring party somewhere in the latitude of Spitsbergen. There was a fair chance of our party going seriously astray as we plunged into the ocean of fog."

Earnest A. Baker 'The British Highlands with Rope and Rucksack' 1933.

The Crazy Pinnacle.
Many people often wonder how this pinnacle on the ridge was so christened. Is it because the shape is crazy or was it once thought that anyone who ventured that way was crazy?
Henry Gale Gotch of the Alpine Club in 1899 suggested that this was "a name given by some poetic or forbidding soul who saw dangers where none exist.

It is a detached mass standing away from the main body of the mountain, and connected therewith by a short but very sharp traverse ridge. There is not the slightest difficulty of ascending it, but apparently the descent to that sharp ridge is alarming to persons of active imagination, for I have known more than one stranded on the top and unable to come down without assistance."

A.P. Abraham in his book 'Beautiful North Wales' quoted an entry in a hotel visitors book
"So and so ascended the Crazy Pinnacle in 5½ minutes and found the rocks very easy.
Below was another entry:-
'Our party descended the Crazy Pinnacle in 5½ seconds and found the rocks very hard'."

Snowdon Guides.
There were many guides operating on Snowdon in the 19th century and the most famous of them all was undoubtedly John Morton who was known as the 'Snowdon Ranger.' In 1854 he declared to George Borrow that the Llyn Cwellyn route which started from his inn was "wonderful for the romantic scenery it affords. From my house you may have the best guide in Wales, whereas the guides of Beddgelert — but I say nothing. If your honour is bound for the Wyddfa, as I suppose you are, you had better start from my house tomorrow under my guidance."

It is possible that the first guide to the Welsh mountains was the one employed by William Johnson, the botanist who paid a visit to the Snowdon area in about 1639. He attempted to persuade his guide to escort him to some steep cliffs in the Carneddau to search for rare plants, but the man refused, expressing a fear of eagles.

William Lloyd, a schoolmaster of Beddgelert was operating as a guide during the period 1790 to 1815 and he was much sought after for his abilities were frequently praised by the travellers who had hired him.

The guides all claimed to know their own special and 'secret' ways of reaching the summit of Snowdon and in the words of Hutton, one of the early mountain visitors this secrecy of route knowledge is emphasised . . . 'the guide did not wish a track, lest the road should be followed by others.' *However the coming of the railways brought so many additional tourists to the area that the once 'secret' paths soon became well trodden tracks.*

The next stage of development of benefit to visitors was the production of Ordnance Survey maps and detailed guidebooks which supplied everyone with information to enable them to make the ascents 'guideless'.

However some of the guides continued to be well employed for many years to come. Robin Hughes of Capel Curig was an old man but he guided Professor John Tyndall and his party to the summit of Snowdon by the Pyg track route in 1860.

The Snowdon Ranger Inn is today a 68 bed Youth Hostel, conveniently situated on the side of the A487 and close to the start of the Snowdon Ranger Track which is still one of the most popular routes to the summit of Snowdon.

One of the earliest inns frequented by visitors to the Snowdonia mountains was the Snowdon Ranger situated on the west side of Snowdon. It was easily reached by rail from Caernarfon or stage coach from Beddgelert and it provided a starting point for one of the easiest ascent routes on Snowdon.

Craddock in 1770 refered to it as a "thatched hut at the foot of the mountain (Snowdon) near a lake which they call Cychwhechlyn (i.e. Quellyn), which I leave you to pronounce as well as you are able."

John Henry Cliffe in his guide book published in 1860 tells us that on the site of the Snowdon Ranger inn there "formerly stood an ancient roadside public house, known as the 'Snowdon Guide.' (The present building was erected by Evan Roberts in the 19th century on the same site. He re-named it the 'Snowdon Ranger'.)

Situated at the foot of Snowdon, the highest peak of which looks less lofty from hence than from the east side — arising, probably, from the greater altitude of the situation — the hotel commands a fine view of Llyn Cwellyn and the magnificent mountains, Mynydd Mawr and Moel Aeliau.

Mr. Evan Roberts, the obliging landlord, is well known on the road between Caernafon and Dolgelley; until lately he drove one of the coaches on this road for many years, and was highly respected. During the summer, in 1857, he provided for the entertainment of his guests, Pugh, the celebrated harper of Corwen, whose dulcet strains upon the three-stringed or Welsh harp — so seldom heard in the Principality — especially Welsh airs, were much and deservedly admired.

The path or pony track from the 'Snowdon Ranger' to the summit of Snowdon is tolerably easy, and many tourists now ascend by this route. In 1857, they generally came from Caernavon under the guidance of a Mr. Homer, who advertised to ascend Snowdon once a week 'weather permitting', by a new route found out by himself, called 'Homer's Route', but which we have reason to believe is much the same as the one followed by the guide from the 'Snowdon Ranger.' At all events it professes to be 'Snowdon made easy'. The charges attendant upon an ascent to the summit of Snowdon from the hotel, are we believe, five shillings for a pony, and seven shillings for a guide: many tourists, however, both ladies and gentlemen, prefer to walk."

John Henry Cliffe. "Notes and recollections of an Angler" 1860.

The Dolbadarn Hotel in Llanberis offered the services of a guide who was described by one of his clients as follows:—

"The guide Robert's costume is rather picturesque and very characteristic, slightly savouring of Switzerland . . . light fawn coloured trousers and vest, no coat; the vest having long arms and fitting to the person. A brigandish hat on his head, a knapsack or large wallet on his shoulders (well strapped over the chest) and a stout stick in his hand . . . Such is honest William Roberts . . . the best recommendation is that he has gone up and over above 2,000 times in the twenty five years of his professional life."

In 1839 William Rowlands, a Llanberis guide who was 81 years of age, took three parties from Llanberis to the summit of Snowdon and back in one day. He then walked over the Llanberis Pass to the Goat hotel at Beddgelert to return a lady's shawl that she had forgotten the previous day.

In 1817 a Beddgelert guide named Lloyd constructed a hut on the summit of Snowdon and obtained a licence to sell alcoholic refreshments there. In later years an old notice board could be seen on the summit bearing the words. "John Roberts, the oldest guide on Snowdon and Philip Williams. Bed, Supper and Breakfast, 5s. MDCCCLV".

Alpine guides were sometimes introduced to the delights of Snowdonia by their wealthy clients who had hired them abroad and persuaded them to come and see the mountains of Britain.

Charles Edward Matthews described an ascent of Snowdon on April 2nd in 1888 as follows:—

"I had with me, as guest, the greatest of Swiss guides, Melchior Anderegg of Meyringen, and he accompanied us on an ascent of Snowdon by way of Grib Goch. I led the way, and as the snow was deep and very soft, it was not an altogether easy task. In one place I hesitated for a few seconds. Melchior instantly forged to the front and proffered his services, which I emphatically declined. 'No,' I said, 'I am guide today, and you are the Herr.' On reaching the summit of Grib Goch, there was the peak of Snowdon on our left, a great white cone rising into blue sky. Melchior, whose knowledge of Swiss distances was faultless, at once said, 'we must go back; we cannot climb the final peak in less than five or six hours.' 'Oh yes,' I said, 'we shall be there in an hour.' 'That sir' was his reply, 'is quite impossible.' In five minutes over the hour we were on top of Snowdon."

When George Borrow asked John Morton, the Snowdon Ranger how many people made the ascent of Snowdon from his house he replied:

"Not as many as I could wish, people in general prefer ascending Snowdon from that trumpery place Beth Gelert; but those who do are fools — begging your honour's pardon. The place to ascend Snowdon from is my house. The way from my house up Snowdon is wonderful for the romantic scenery which it affords; that from Beth Gelert can't be named in the same day with it for scenery; moreover, from my house you may have the best guide in Wales; whereas the guides of Beth-Gelert — but I say nothing. If your honour is bound for the Wyddfa, as I suppose you are, you had better start from my house tomorrow under my guidance."

A train descending from Snowdon summit, near Hebron Station.

The Snowdon Mountain Railway.
The Snowdon mountain Railway has the distinction of being the only rack and pinion railway in Britain. It was opened in 1896 and is still worked by steam. The line is 4¾ miles long and has a gauge of 2' 7½". The gradients are never steeper than 1 in 5½ (whereas the gradients on Swiss mountain railways are as much as 1 in 2) and the sharpest curve is 264' radius which may

be compared with 100′ radius in Switzerland. Construction of the Snowdon railway was undertaken by the engineers Sir Douglas and Francis Fox of Westminster.

Passengers travelling the line in 1904 would have paid 3/6 for a single journey to the summit and 2/6 for a descent. Return fare was 5/-. If you only wished to travel half way it cost 2/-single and 3/- return.

It cost 6d to telephone the summit. Trains were run and the hotel opened from Easter to the end of October. If you wished to leave your bicycle at Llanberis station it would cost you fourpence.

The ruination of Snowdon.
"Above all should the summits themselves be kept sacred and their noble lineaments undisfigured. The only mountain that has so far fallen helplessly a prey to the general despoiler in Snowdon, and the deflowering of Snowdon was such an ugly deed that it has remained a warning for the last forty years. I well remember how the news that a chief promoter of the railway to the summit had been killed in a trial journey was received by lovers of the mountain with bloodthirsty resignation. But the evil that men do lives after them. The huddle of shacks still graces the tip of Eryri, the place of eagles, sung by the birds, the symbol of ancient glories."

Ernest A. Baker. 'The British Highlands with Rope and Rucksack' 1923.

Before his time.
George Borrow would certainly not have used the Snowdon railway if it had been there in his time for he once said. "I despise railroads and those who travel by them."

Beware of tourists.
"The steam railway from Llanberis to the summit of Y Wyddfa, unsightly though it is has served one good purpose. It has concentrated the ordinary tourist and the excursionist upon the least interesting side, and left the climber in undisturbed possession of the wilder parts of the mountain. Were it not for this fact, the ever-increasing hordes that over-run Snowdon during the summer months would compel the climber to desert it and seek less frequented cliffs. Only those who have attempted the ascent of Clogwyn y Garnedd gullies on a fine August or September afternoon can quite appreciate what a source of danger the British tourist is. As Mr. Pilkington says in Mountaineering (Badminton Series), 'No amount of climbing skill or precaution will save you from a well-aimed gingerbeer bottle'."

'Climbers Club Journal' 1898.

On the other hand. . .
"There is a vague impression abroad, and I must confess to having once felt something of the kind myself, that the Snowdon railway would in some sort spoil the mountain, that its solitudes would be desecrated and shaken by the perpetual roar and clatter of a noisy locomotive. As for this little midget, it seems to me a trifle scarcely worth considering except for the pleasure it gives to innumerable people who are still possessed of all their faculties, have eyes and brains and every necessary qualification to enable them to enjoy the noblest view in Britain, but purchance no longer be able to climb 3500 feet without injury or discomfort'."

A.G. Bradley 'Highways and Byeways' in North Wales.

Playing safe.
" 'Of the Snowdon Mountain Railway, I will say only that it was opened in 1896, and that it has carried to the top a great number of people, most of whom would not have missed it if they had never been. I knew a man who made the excursion once; when the train got to the top, it was in mist as usual, and he thought there would be nothing to see and might be a precipice about, so he sat in the train till it went down again'."

Patrick Monkhouse. 'On foot in North Wales'. 1934.

When to ascend Snowdon.
" 'Go when you can, but if possible, choose well the time of your going. Go in the broad daylight; also, go through the night and arrive at the summit in time to see the sun rise. Go when the full moon is shining and go on a night when all the lamps of heaven are studding the velvet blackness of the sky, and sparkling in the mountain tarns. And go when you are old, or when time and conditions compel you, by the evening train of the Snowdon Mountain Railway, to spend the hours of fading light watching the sunset, and the period of night listening to wireless entertainment from America in the hotel near the summit, or in your own tent, and then emerge to greet the dawn from the crest of Y Wyddfa, before descending to mundane matters.'

If you would see Snowdon in all aspects of his grandeur do not confine your visits to warm August afternoons when the still warm air rests around the tawny slumbering lion — a seemingly old, toothless and circus suppressed lion. No, Snowdon does not show you all his qualities in that slumberous condition.

Come at least once in each month of the year, if you are able. If not, come when the mountain is dancing with the coming of Spring; come when its lush slopes are blooming with the wealth of summer; come when October rains show what rain really means and Snowdon's slopes are 'nothing but streams'; come, also, in the clear crisp winter air when Snowdon wears his robe of spotless snow, and early evening starlight glints on the snow cornices of his ancient crown.

Yes, come, and you shall see wonders."
Valentine Davies 'A Guide to Snowdon' 1936.

Gully climbing in Snowdon.
Bryant's Gully 1899.
First climbed not surprisingly by G.B. Bryant and party.
"A brief lunch was disposed of in a small hollow. We shared it with a well nourished and contented looking toad, living there in apparent freedom from all family cares. The general verdict was that, whilst containing nothing to attract seekers after glory, yet it was an excellent gully."

Jammed Boulder Gully.
Climbed by J.M.A. Thompson and R. Williams in 1900.
"The exit is narrow, and the arrival of corpulent or clumsy followers will be watched with amusement by those who have gone before. A commodious theatre is provided for the spectacle."

Schoolmasters' Gully.
Climbed in 1906 by H. Mitchell, A.E. Baker, W.J. Drew and G.T. Atchinson.
"Each of us insisted that the man before him made a ridiculous fuss and spent an absurdly long time over it. Criticism and advice followed freely but each of us modified his opinion when his own turn came."

Great Gully.
"This is the most popular climb on Snowdon . . . A chaos of boulders leads to a short easy chimney pitch, and the bed of the gully continues fairly steeply ahead until the notorious cave pitch demands attention. A great boulder spans the gully and there is no difficulty in scrambling up into the cave below it; where a glimmer of light is seen up above; this comes from a funnel like hole which affords access to the screes above. One of the pioneers said that this place could only be negotiated by 'an indescribable twist of the body,' which is difficult to understand nowadays, for the passage is easy, being well lubricated with slimy moisture. The exit from the hole has been found to be blackened with various articles of domestic economy from the summit hotel. An indescribable twist of the tongue would facilitate matters if a wire mattress or a wheel-barrow are encountered. Above this pitch the gully becomes shallow, and

after working out leads somewhat indefinitely up to the summit."
George D. Abraham. 'British Mountain Climbs' 1909.

Public attention was first drawn to Lliwedd as a climbing ground by the ascent in 1883 by Messrs T.W. Wall and A.H. Stocker, and thus described by the former in the Alpine Journal:—

"The northern face consists of four buttresses, with three fairly well-defined couloirs between them. The summit ridge has two peaks, of which the western, nearer Snowdon, is the higher by a few feet. In January 1882 from the summit of Grib Goch Mr. A.H. Stocker and myself were struck by the grand appearance of the Lliwedd cliffs, and hearing from Owen, the landlord of the Pen-y-gwryd Hotel, that the northern face had never been climbed, the desire to make the first ascent naturally came upon us. On the 10th we made our first attempt by the central couloir, which leads up to the depression between the two summits. As it was raining the whole day the rocks were in an abominable state, and it was with the greatest difficulty that we managed to get up about 150 feet".

The 800 foot cliffs of Lliwedd where the early climbers pioneered an intricate network of routes on loose and vegetated rock. In Slanting Gully at mid-height is the mythical cave where King Arthur and his knights are said to be still sleeping after a bivouac of thirteen centuries. It is known as Ogof Arthur.

Slanting Gully of Lliwedd — early soloing.
"On Thursday, August 30, 1894, this gully cost a valuable life. Mr. J. Mitchell of Oxon, an assistant editor of the 'New Historical English Dictionary,' started from the foot at about 2.00 p.m. The first pitch was quickly ascended, and he then proceeded, apparently without difficulty, to the foot of the long chimney, which he passed by means of the face. On reaching the top he waved his hankerchief, and, being asked what it was like, he replied that it was very stiff. Not long afterwards he was seen in a cave, which the lookers-on (probably in error) identified with the highest point reached by previous climbers. From this he climbed with great difficulty to the top, as it appeared from below, of a long chasm, with his head just below an overhanging rock, upwards of 150 ft. above the cave, and after more than half an hour of fruitless endeavour to make further progress he fell at 4.30 p.m., and was killed on the spot.

The body was found at the above mentioned cave, and was brought down by four quarrymen at great personal risk. The lesson which should be drawn from this is, that if a man will insist on climbing alone he should not choose for his attack, climbs which parties of greater skill and experience than his own have found to be beyond their powers.''

W.P. Haskett Smith. 'Climbing in the British Isles' Vol. II 1895.

Success in Slanting Gully.
''The last swing out on to the slab on the left tested the arms terribly, for the feet flew back into space; there was a strange sensation of emulating a fly crawling along a ceiling. Gravitation created an ugly backward pull until the body could be raised and steadied to balance on a small foothold on the slab. Several excrescences gave splendid help; the fingers gripped exultingly in a deeper crevice behind some wedged boulders. The Slanting Gully was conquered.''

George D. Abraham 1897.

The Climbing Parson.
"During our stay at Pen-y-gwryd a few years ago we made the aquaintance of a gentleman, a clergyman of the Church of England, who was possessed with a most extraordinary mania for climbing mountains. He would make, for instance, Pen-y-gwryd, Capel Curig, Llanberis, and several other stations in Snowdonia, his headquarters for a week or ten days, until, in fact he had 'exhausted the scenery.' Picture to yourself a tall man, about fifty-two years of age, of a wiry, spare habit, rather slightly built, dressed in a pair of dingy slop trousers, a linen spencer of the same complexion, without hat or covering of any sort for the head, no neck-tie, his shirt collar unbuttoned, with an enormous Alpenstock or climbing pole, seven or eight feet in length, in his hand, and you may perhaps be able to form some idea of the strange grotesque figure we have endeavoured to describe. His object was, to use his own expression, 'to follow the sky line' of every mountain he visited. For example he would ascend Snowdon from Llanberis, but instead of following the beaten track, he would take the edge of the mountain along the verge of the highest precipices, following what he called the 'sky line' until he reached the summit; he would then descend the other side of the mountain to Beddgelert, in a similar manner. He most frequently performed his excursions alone, although occasionally, when not so familiar with the locality, he availed himself of the services of a guide. He would follow up these rambles de die in diem, regardless of the weather, and was generally on his legs from about 9 a.m. until 8 p.m. The most extraordinary thing was, how he could keep up such violent daily exercise without any refreshment whatever during the period he was among the mountains. To prevent thirst, he carried a small pebble in his mouth; and Henry Owen, the guide, assured us that he never saw him partake of anything to eat or drink, not even a cup of cold water whilst on an excursion.

We have several times met him on his return to the inn, drenched with perspiration, and whilst his dinner was being prepared, he would continue at gentle exercise (staff in hand) to 'cool down' — like a race-horse after a 'breather' — preparatory to partaking of his repast — in fine weather generally alfresco — exhibiting not the least apparent fatigue. He was a man of very temperate habits: two or three glasses of sherry were the extent of his libatations; he avoided smoking, and he would be up early in the morning performing his ablutions for several hours. He appeared to have no other object in climbing to the wild mountain tops than merely (as he said) to behold the wonderful works of the Almighty. Such was the remarkable individual with whom we became acquainted at Pen-y-gwryd. We found him a most refined, intellectual companion, well read and informed on all subjects of general interest, thoroughly versed in Welsh topography, and in his demeanour most affable and courteous. He informed us that he spent several weeks annually in North Wales, following up the same pursuit mountain climbing, either revisiting old scenes, or finding out, if possible, some fresh mountain path still more difficult and arduous to surmount than what he had previously attempted. In following the 'sky line,' no rocks, however rough, no precipices — unless perfectly inaccessible ever daunted him. This singular mania or hobby horse, he appears to have followed up for years, and continued with unabated ardour. The last time we saw him was on a wet, stormy morning, preparing to 'hie away to the mountain's brow,' on his route to Pen-y-Gwryd to Capel Curig; the said route being the 'sky line' over the summit and entire length of the lofty Moel Siabod."

John Henry Cliffe. 'Notes and Recollections of an Angler'. 1860.

The Parson's Nose to the north east of Crib y ddysgl. It is possible that the 'climbing parson' made the first ascent of this rock in 1850. Photo — George & Ashley Abraham.

The Parson's Nose.
"It is a spur of Crib-y-Ddysgl and is easily identified by its projecting in a northerly direction between the two little pools in Cwm Glas. No one seems to know the origin of the name; possibly it may have been scaled by the famous climbing cleric who haunted Snowdonia half a century ago."

W.P. Haskett Smith. 1895.

Hard to locate in the mist.
"We spent a long day in cloud searching all round Cwm Glas for the reputed Parson's Nose; and the mists opening a window below us, suddenly framed a rock profile projecting from the crag, an aquiline episcopal nose of the haught Wellesley type. We never could find it again; but it seemed then as though Snowdon had been sealed mysteriously to holy order."

Geoffrey Winthrop Young. 1927.

A similar experience.
"Snowdon's many heads were muffled in cloud when we set out from Gorphwysfa across the tangle of cliffs and screes where Crib Goch breaks down in ruin, and to find the Parson's Nose was a problem requiring not only map and compass, and skill in using them, but also local experience. As we weathered buttress after buttress and picked our way through innumerable breaches in the face of the mountain, it was as much a matter of estimating height and distance by our sense of exertion as of identifying landmarks. In time, we found ourselves entering a big hollow, in the midst of which a stream came down out of the invisible. The girdling cliffs we could not see, but we felt that they were there: in the heart of such a cwm, the echoes of tumbling water and the movement of the wind conspire to make the unseen palpable, as if one sent out magic feelers into the obscurity.

What we could not be sure of was whether this was Cwm Glas, or whether we had strayed into the lesser hollow of Cwm Glas Bach. Anon we stopped on the shores of a pool, whose phantasmal waters spread away without any distinguishable limit; we might have been standing beside a lake of vast extent, had there been such a thing so high in the mountains. We had however, not long to wait for the mist to break; the dramatic moment came 'There's the nose!' someone shouted; and over our shoulders, in the opposite direction to where we had looked for it, the great sweeping profile, the ghost of a mighty cliff, loomed through the shifting vapours, itself scarce more substantial. Our pool was but a little one after all, though the mist had made it sea-like."

Earnest A. Baker. 'The British Highlands with Rope and Rucksack' 1923.

The psychology of mist.
"Mist may not break down the climber's morale by force and battery as the wind does; its methods are more cunning, more subtly contrived: a kind of psychological warfare which slowly undermines his confidence and steals away his resolution. Fog sneaks upon him, carressingly, twining his senses into knots, rubbing shoulders like a false friend and whispering lies. It is a familiar spirit, a brooding presence, plying his mind with fancies which are not of his creation. It shuts him off from the world and having got him to itself preys on his imagination. A man is never so utterly alone as when the clouds come down and leave him groping on a mountainside . . . Its clammy presence damps down the spirit, Its murkiness baffles the eyes, like frosted glass. Its voices are neither here nor there. Even when one is tolerably certain of one's bearings, it can be very depressing to have to keep on hour after hour with nothing to see but a changeless swirl and always at the back of the mind the childish dread of being lost. Sooner or later claustrophobia sets in."

W.K. Richmond, 'Climber's Testament' 1950.

"The mists that round you peak concentrating spread,
Changes partend that mountain-dwellers dread
Clouds, dense and lowering, throng the western sky."

Lord Byron.

Llanberis Pass.

'When we came to the top of Nant Gwynant, we quitted the road and passed over some bogs to the side of the mountain on our right. Winding along this, and turning to the right, we entered the pass by a miserable horse path, which winds among the rocks, high above the bottom. Half a mile further the road begins to descend in the opposite direction. This part called Gorphwysfa, (the Resting Place), is the head of the Vale of Llanberis, though it does not take that name for some distance. Without having witnessed it, scarcely any idea can be formed of the terrific grandeur of this pass, which continues undiminished for three miles. On each side, rocks tower upon rocks to an immense height, receding but little; and the enormous masses scattered in the bottom have so evidently fallen from these stupendous precipices, that in passing under them, the mind of the beholder is unvoluntarily impressed with dread, lest the overhanging rocks should lose their hold, and, in an instant, crush him to atoms.'

Thomas Compton 1814.

The Llanberis Pass from near Pen y pass. The crag Dinas y Cromlech can be seen on the rignt.

"In the pass of Llanberis there are those portentuous boulders by the roadside at Pont y Gromlech (and what an earth-shaking roar they must have made when they tore loose from their sockets, vaulting and rebounding to this last resting place of theirs!), yet nowadays the bus-loads go by sedately and never see anything more alarming than a mild landslip."

W.K. Richmond. 'Climbers Testament'. 1950.

Hetty of the Cromlech Boulders once resided in the Llanberis Pass. It is said that she used the huge Cromlech boulders as a shelter while she looked after her cows in the summer and a patch of land here is still referred to as Hetty's Island.

Caddy of Cwm Glas was another interesting woman who lived in the Llanberis Pass. She was known as "the woman with the beard who was feared by children from Capel Curig to Caernarvon." *She was also a well known wrestler.*

Margaret Uch Evan was a remarkable woman who once lived in a cottage on the edge of Llyn Peris. Pennant did not meet her on his famous tour of Wales but he wrote the following description of her amazing strength and abilities.

"She is at this time (1786) about ninety years of age. This extraordinary female was the greatest hunter, shooter, and fisher of her time. She kept a dozen at least of dogs . . . killed more foxes in one year than all the confederate hunts do in ten: rowed stoutly, and was queen of the lake: fiddled excellently, and knew all our old music . . . was a good joiner: and at the age of seventy, was the best wrestler in the country, and few young men dared try a fall with her . . . Margaret was also a blacksmith, shoe-maker, boat builder, and maker of harps. She shoed her own horses, made her own shoes, and built her own boats, while she was under contract to carry the copper ore down the lakes."

Dinas Cromlech in the Llanberis Pass — one of the 'Three Cliffs' where the first routes were pioneered by John Menlove Edwards in the 1930's. The Central feature is the open book corner which was first climbed by Joe Brown in 1952. He christened the route Cenotaph Corner and it was a follow up to a route to the right which was called Cemetery Gates.

Snowdon run.
Chris Preston in 1945 heard that someone had run up Snowdon from Llanberis in less than an hour.

'So after a day's climbing he ate a large steak pudding and ran up in 48 minutes and down in 26 and a ¼.'

Inns of the Snowdon mountain men.

"I came up to the top of the pass where two inns stand together in mist, friendly as all places are which promise fire and food in the mountains. They are interesting inns. Their kind in Scotland have improbable trout and salmon stuffed in the hall with the name of the man who caught them in 1899. But these inns at the foot of Snowdon preserve other relics. They have shelves stacked with enormous nailed boots, ice-axes, ropes.

Their halls ring to the tramp of mountaineers and in the evening men talk of nothing but 'couloirs' and 'chimneys' and 'glaciers' and other things which mean nothing to men who do not venture into high places. The shadow of Snowdon is always on the Pass of Llanberis."

H.V. Morton 'In search of Wales' 1932.

Today the Pen-y-Pass Inn no longer serves alcoholic refreshment to thirsty mountaineers for it has been converted into a superior grade youth hostel with extensions to the extensions. As a starting point for an ascent of Snowdon it is more popular than ever and you have to arrive early to obtain a parking place.

Verses from "The Pen-y-Pass Song"
"The mountains of youth have all vanished, they say,
But I know the lie of them still;
Just turn to the right at the end of the day,
And stop at the top of the hill,
'Tis there you will find it, its beds and its brass
When Christmas has come to your call:
For the mountains are waiting round dear Pen-y-Pass,
And the grey sky is over it all.
While the wind from Cwm Idwal, Cwm Llydau, Cwm Glas,
Comes welcoming over the scree:
"Come back, mountain friends, to your Rest on the Pass;
Come back, mountain climber, to me."

Our cairns for the bairns of the future may last
As signs of the climbs of our day;
But we hear the cheer of our friends of the past
In the dark, as a mark for our way.
Though memory calls us, 'its memory of joys
Ere sorrow joined fun in our sack;
And the thoughts that we shared with each other as boys
Are the thoughts that old Snowdon brings back.

And the wind from Cwm Idwal, Cwm Llydau, Cwm Glas,
Comes whispering over the scree:
"Comes back, mountain friends, to your youth on the pass;
Come home, mountain climber, to me."

G. Winthrop Young: Pen-y-Pass, December 1913.

Today the Pen-y-Gwryd is owned by Chris Briggs who has been here for many years and has played a leading role in mountain rescue in the area.

The Pen-y-Gwryd Hotel.

"The inn is happily situate at the junction of three roads, severally leading to Beddgelert, Llanberis, and Capel Curig. It is literally an oasis in the wilderness, a palm tree in the desert, a solitary spot of verdue, snatched by the industry of man from the wreck of nature; and notwithstanding its elevation — for it is oftentimes in the clouds — and its exposure to the frosts and snows of winter, you will observe several kinds of garden flowers and vegetables flourishing luxuriantly; and hereafter we have little doubt that human industry will further improve the outdoor character of the place . . . The inn is situate at the foot of those lofty sterile mountains, Glyder Vawr and Bach, the ascent to the summits of which forms a delightful excursion. Then there is the ascent to Snowdon, by Llyn Llydaw and Glas Llyn the 'Azure Lake', under the awful precipices of Moel y Wyddfa, 'one of the finest scenes in Britain' — a scene of stupendous grandeur and fearful sublimity, in some respects unequalled in Wales."

John Henry Cliffe. 'Notes and recollections of an Angler' 1860.

By the shore of Llyn Ogwen. In the distance can be seen Ogwen Cottage with Y Garn on the left and Foel goch to the right.

Elidir Fawr.

The ancient name of this mountain is Carnedd Elidir which is believed to commemorate Elidir Mwynfawr a North Country Briton who married Eurgain, a daughter of Maelgwyn Gwynedd. It is said that Elidir owned a remarkable horse which could carry a load of seven and a half persons, consisting of himself, his wife and five of his followers. His jester ran at his side and held on to the saddle to form the half person.

"Most British hills are so complex in their make-up as to defy all but the most expert analysis. A few hundred yards on the crest of Elidir, for example, will reveal the wierdest assortment — grits and shales, boulders of green agglomerate rifted with marble and felspar, leaves of purplish slate, sulphur coloured blocks and laval ashes with nuggets and bubukles embedded in them — bits and pieces of all shapes and sizes strewn around like the debris of some unearthly explosion."

W.K. Richmond. 'Climbers Testament'. 1950.

Y Garn

"She sits in splendour, great against the sky,
And broods upon the little ways of men:
Her mighty knees reach down to meet the road
Where men and horses, sheep and barking dogs
Pass every day without a look for her
Who holds in the wide lap they cannot see
A secret tarn like the dim eye of God
Wet for the sorrows of the world he made."

E.H. Young.

The Glyders.

A day on the Glyders can be regarded as a very special experience, particularly if your route started with an ascent of the North Ridge of Tryfan and was subsequently followed by a scramble up the Bristly Ridge to gain the summit plateau of Glyder Fach. From there one may have the pleasure of visiting the Cantilever Stone, Glyder Fach summit, Castell y Gwynt and Glyder Fawr summit, before dropping down via the Devil's Kitchen track to the shores of Llyn Idwal, passing the impressive sweep of the Idwal Slabs where climbers are swarming in the sun, like ants, taking their pleasure from one hunk of rock, whilst you on your walk have handled thousands of rocks and enjoyed a rewarding day.

Llyn Bochllwyd and Glyder Fach. George and Ashley Abraham.

Excursion to the summit of Glyder Fach in 1860.

Glyder Fawr and Glyder Bach are two of the loftiest and most rugged mountains in Snowdonia; the former, according to the latest survey, being 3,300 feet, and the latter, 3,000 feet above the level of the sea.

The frosts and rains of ages, combined with other elemental agency, have operated upon the external face of these elevated mountains. Rocks have been shivered to pieces, huge masses or protuberances, called 'horns,' stand out occasionally from the sides of the mountains, and fragments of rocks of all sizes strew the sides and bottom, which renders progress at times painful and difficult. This is one of the sternest regions of desolation in Britain — a wilder or more impressive scene imagination cannot perceive.

The morning proved exceedingly favourable for our projected ascent. Huge masses of clouds, some of which slightly rested on the summit of the mountain, with occasional bursts of sunshine, and a gentle breeze, the bracing and invigorating effects of which greatly assisted us in our progress, left nothing that could be desired. At nine o'clock a.m. the order was given to march and accompanied by our 'compagnons de voyage,' two friends, and our guide, Henry Owen, we started on this most interesting excursion. Previously to leaving home, we had made a rough pen and ink sketch of the engraving in Pennant's tour of the tall 'columnar stones' on the summit of Glyder Bach, to test the accuracy of the description given in the text: this, we need hardly say, was fully realized; not a stone moved out of its place since Pennant's visit nearly eighty years before. After leaving Pen y Gwryd, our route lay over a peat morass, through which flowed the Gwryd on its course to the Llyniau Mymbyr, commonly called the Capel Curig Lakes. After crossing the river we soon commenced the ascent of the mountain, which though rough, was less toilsome upon the whole than we expected. After proceeding slowly for at least two hours, we neared the summit, and resting for a brief interval under one of the 'horns' refreshed ourselves with some deliciously cold pure spring water; which slightly flavoured with cognac, proved very refreshing. The water we partook of flowed, or rather welled, out from the mountainside, creating one of those green oases so pleasing to the eye amidst the ventureless waste — with eternal barreness and desolation around it. Here we paused to survey the grand array of huge mountains, which rise up and encompass this elevated region in almost every direction. Amongst the chief attractions of this magnificent scene was Snowdon and his attendant Alps; the lovely Nant Gwynant, and its lake; Moel Siabod, 'its sides and base covered with verdure, its upper part a great pile of broken rocks;' and the lakes and mountains in the neighbourhood of Capel Curig. We now gradually neared the area on the summit, which we found covered with groups of columnar stones, some of vast size, from ten to thirty feet long, lying in all directions. The scene before us, in fact, resembled the ruins of some vast 'Druidical Temple' — a mountain 'Stonehenge' — which had been overthrown ages ago by some awful convulsion of nature. Indeed so strong was our impression that we were in the midst of venerable Druidical remains, that it was some time ere we could convince ourselves that what we saw was in reality a chaotic mass of stones thrown into inconceivable confusion — the work of time and the violence of the elements.

"Pennant's description is so truthful, that we cannot do better than give it. 'I climbed up,' say he, 'one of these stones, twenty-five feet long and six broad, and stamping it with my foot, felt a strong trembulous motion from end to end. Another, eleven feet and six in circumference, was poised so nicely in the thinnest part on the point of a rock, that to the appearance, the touch of a child would overset it. One side of the mountain is formed into a gap, with sharp rocks pointing upwards to a great height.' The stone Pennant alluded to lies in a horizontal position, supported by nine or ten upright stones, forming a sort of natural altar.

On this stone we also climbed, and stood with reverential feelings on the very point of the stone that this eminent topographer and antiquary trod full eighty winters before. This natural carnedd of columnar stones would appear to be of basaltic formation, as other portions of the steep sides of Glyder Vawr, overhanging the Pass of Llanberis, 'exhibit ranges of basaltic rocks, much convulsed, and one columnar cluster stands apart from the rest, quite upright.' Several rocky fragments which have fallen down into the Pass are described as being sixty feet in length, exhibiting 'marvellous variations in colouring and outline.'

'It is a barren scene, and wild,
Where naked cliffs are rudely piled.'

Having spent nearly an hour in the examination of this wonderful world of nature, we proceeded to the northern side of Glyder Bach, from whence we had a sort of bird's eye view of the summit of Trifaen."

John Henry Cliffe. 'Notes and Recollections of an Angler'. 1860.

The Cantilever Stone on Glyder Fach with author Chris Barber testing the vibrations. 'As there was no one around to hold the camera or pose for me, I had to use a tripod, set off the delayed action and hastily scramble into position — just in time to hear the shutter go click.'

Glyder Fach or Glyder Fawr?

"Glyder Fach though called 'the lesser' is far finer that its brother peak, so much so that many have found great difficulty in believing that the Ordnance Surveyors were right in ascribing 17′ of superiority to the more lumpy western summit. One might be tempted to build a 20′ cairn but for fear of spoiling the great glory of Glyder Fach, the chaos of rocks on its summit. The present cairn was not in existence ten years ago, and must have been built about 1887.

Directly under the top stone is the minimum thermometer, which has been kept there for some years. The most interesting thing on the whole mountain is undoubtedly the pile of stones on the top. According to the bard Taliesin it is the burial place of a mighty warrior, one Eidiw. If a kind of Stonehenge was erected there to his memory and afterwards got upset by an earthquake it might account for present appearances. Edward Lhwyd, the great antiquary, was particularly struck by them 200 years ago, and his description and remarks are equally applicable to-day.

'On the utmost top of the Glyder,' he says, 'I observed prodigious heaps of stones, many of the longeness of those of Stonehenge, but of all the irregular shapes imaginable, and all lying in confusion as the ruins of any building can be supposed to do . . . Had they been in a valley I had concluded they had fallen from the neighbouring rocks . . . but, being on the highest part of the hill, they seemed to me much more remarkable.'

'Lhwyd's description fired the curiosity of the travellers who explored Wales nearly a century later, and the amusing part of it is that they could not find this wonderful mountain or even hear of it from the intelligent natives."

W.P. Haskett Smith. 'Climbing in the British Isles'. Vol II 1895.

The chaotic mass of boulders marking the summit of Glyder Fach.

Once there were giants in the land.

"What random reason can explain why the summit of Glyder Fach should be piled high with massive blocks and cantilevers, as if some Gargantua of the troll-world had once upon a time set his heart on erecting the cairn of all cairns . . . The atmosphere of the place is haunted still, as if the ogre had only recently been called away and might as suddenly return."

W.K. Richmond. 'Climbers Testament'. 1950.

"In one place, the colossal blocks and splinters have built themselves up into the semblance of a fort. Crowned with flat slabs, from the vantage of which one could fancy a Welsh Kinglet of old making his last stand against invaders. Legend has it that this is the burial-mound of an ancient warrior."

Earnest A. Baker. 'The British Highlands with Rope and Rucksack'. 1923.

Glyder Fawr and Glyder Fach — A question of height!

"Glyder Fawr (3279′) and Glyder Fach (3262′) are separated by a long mile and a dip of less than 200 feet. Many people consider the Fach the finer mountain, by virtue of its extraordinary top, and a few cling to the belief that the surveyors were wrong and it is really the higher."

Patrick Monkhouse. 'On foot in North Wales'. 1934.

Bristly Ridge.
"To find the top of the Bristly Ridge of Glyder Fach in mist, at dusk, alone, and come down it, was an adventure that nothing in later mountaineering could surpass. The curlews wailing over the swamps, sheep coughing invisibly out of the greyness on the chilly flats, the pinnacles of the ridge looking enormous and the wind whistling through the broken wall on Bwlch Tryfan were impressions that stamped themselves deeper than the memory."

Dorothy Pilley. Climbing Days.

"At the east end (of Glyder Fach) is the bristly ridge leading down to Bwlch Tryfan. This is stimulating, but not difficult."

W.P. Haskett Smith. 'Climbing in the British Isles'. Vol II 1895.

Castell y Gwynt — Castle of the Winds on the south west side of Glyder Fach summit.

Castell y Gwynt (Castle of the Winds).
"The castell, which is at the junction of the two Glyders, can be seen, it is said from Bangor and Beaumaris, and even from Cader Idris. The castell is sometimes mistaken for the summit and climbed in vain — except, indeed, to see its extraordinary rockwork!"

'Gossiping Guide to Wales'. 1904.

Afairy fortress.
"It was 4 p.m. when we scrambled on to the summit plateau between castell y Gwynt and Glyder Fawr to find a scene of imaginable beauty before us. Castell y Gwynt, the Castle of the Winds, was transformed into a fairy fortress with the snow plastered rocks glittering in the golden-red light of the setting sun, while the snow on the plateau was frozen into a brilliant sea of ripples shadowed now by the low sun and thrown into relief."

Nea Morin. 'A Woman's Reach'. 1968.

From Glyder Fawr — a view of enchantment.

"The view was inspiriting. As far as the eye could see, it was all one ocean of silver cumulus, unbroken save for the higher peaks which figured upon it as on an island in an archipelago. Detached from its base, the conical stack of Y Wyddfa floated serenely, looking like another St. Kilda. Moel Siabod was an iceberg; and in the far distance Cader and Arenig were viking ships breasting the wavy horizon. This inland sea extended over the whole of North Wales and far into England, where doubtless it appeared as an overcast sky. How prosaic! and how privileged I was to be the sole witness of so much splendour. Millions lay buried on the floor of that sea and just then I would not have changed places with any one of them."

W.K. Richmond. 'Climbers Testament'. 1950.

Self-help.

"On May 17, 1908, Baron Vaon Hobn set out from Pen-y-Gwyryd to ascend the Glyder Fawr, and reached in a mist, what he took to be its summit. It is practically certain that he was in reality, not far distant on Castell-y-Gwynt, when a rock he had touched came down, causing him to fall and fracture his leg. There he remained all night, vainly expecting to be rescued. When daylight broke, he fashioned a splint from his walking stick, reserving the crook to aid his descent. The whole day was employed in working slowly and painfully downwards in a recumbent posture, his only food being a morsel of chocolate. A second night was spent without victuals on the mountainside. On the morning of the third day his shouts were answered by the barking of dogs, which had the effect of stirring the inmates of the hotel to activity. He had almost completed the descent, being near the stone wall, when help at length was brought. So notable an instance of perseverance and resourcefulness in a grave dilemma must not be allowed to pass into oblivion."

W.P. Haskett Smith. 'Climbing in the British Isles'. Vol II 1895.

Mist widows.

"Ye rash men who go up the Glyders
Not one of you ever considers
If you see a thick fog when
You start from Lake Ogwen
Your wives may be changed into widders."

Visitors' book at Ogwen Cottage.

Cwm Idwal.

". . . a fit place to inspire murderous thoughts, environed with horrible precipices, shading a lake, lodged in its bottom. The shepherds' fable that it is the haunt of deamons; and that no bird dare fly over its damned water, fatal as that of Avernus.

Observe on the right, a stupendous 'roche fendue,' or, split rock, called Twll-du and the 'Devil's Kitchen' . . . On surmounting all my difficulties, and taking a little breath, I ventured to look down this dreadful apeture, and found its horrors far from being lessened, in my exalted situation."

Thomas Pennant. 'A Tour in Wales'. 1781.

"The Devil's Kitchen is one of the most notorious climbs in North Wales and deserves its ill-fame. It is the great cleft up in the decaying limestone wall above Llyn Idwal, a dark dank, noisome ravine with slimy rotting cliffs echoing at all seasons with the slash of its waterfall, an ill-omened place associated with fatal accidents and daunting escapes from disaster.

At the door of the kitchen one goes into shadow and the huge, bulging 400 feet walls seem to hang over one threateningly. Daylight comes down through the scimitor-shaped gap above and you make a watery way over a large jammed boulder and up by a semi-detached pinnacle from which the inner recesses and the climb itself are revealed."

Dorothy Pilley. 'Climbing Days'. 1935.

△ Lliwedd from Llyn Teyrn.

Snowdon from the Pyg Track. ▽

The lower pitch, Devil's Kitchen.

George and Ashley Abraham.

The Devil's Kitchen.

"Twll Du the 'notoriously dangerous rift in the crags between Glyder Fawr and Y Garn. The writer would urge that the complete ascent should be left severely alone. Recent fatal accidents confirm the opinion that it is not a justifiable climb by reason of the peculiarly unreliable nature of the rock."

George D. Abraham. 'British Mountain Climbs'. 1909.

Looking through the Devil's Kitchen to view Llyn Idwal directly below and Llyn Ogwen in the distance.

It must be emphasised that the Devil's Kitchen track does not go down the centre of the fissure, but it follows a diagonal line down to pass below the great cleft. Numerous walkers over the years have foolishly tried to descend the actual Devil's Kitchen in error with disastrous results.

∆ Early morning on Crib-y-ddysgl.

Approaching Castell-y-Gwynt and Glyder Fach. ∇

The Idwal slabs in Cwm Idwal.

The ascent of the Devil's Kitchen was attempted as far back as 1865 by an 'anonymous contributor to Chamber's Journal.'

"In 1898 two climbers suceeded in wet weather in ascending the south wall, effecting probably for the first time, an exit by the rocks. The wall was attacked just above the second pitch, and scaled for fifty feet to a small green patch, where the rope can be secured. A bulge on the right was crossed to a narrow horizontal ledge, which leads to a short chimney beside overhanging rock at the top of the pitch. The wall has been descended more than once and ascended many times — on one occasion by a climber single-handed, whose time, taken by friends below was exactly fifteen minutes.

The wall is composed of treacherous limestone, with undiscoverable defects in regard to texture. It is therefore dangerous and unsuitable for ascent. Moreover, the climb possesses no good quality in which it is not surpassed by others equally accessible from Ogwen.

Recent falls of rock have brought considerable changes. More light penetrates, and lessens the weird solemnity natural to the cleft."

J.M. Archer Thompson. 'Climbing in the Ogwen District'. 1910.

"In 1895, the waterfall froze, and Archer Thompson and another man made an astonishing climb up it cutting steps in the ice with Mrs. Jones's coal hatchet. The climb (which took seven hours) is recorded in Thompson's 'Climbing in the Ogwen District.' He concludes 'sooner or later the exceptional conditions must recur, and these details may then interest those who have the good fortune to repeat the ascent in the manner described.' So far as I know, however, it has never been done again."

Patrick Monkhouse. 'On Foot in North Wales'. 1934.

The right hand wall of the Devil's Kitchen was first climbed by Colin Kirkus in 1934. It is seldom climbed today. The right entrance wall was climbed in 1969 by Ken Hopkiss, Roger Lovill and Tom Leppert using artificial aids. They named their route 'The Devil Rides Out' and graded it Hard Very Severe/A3.

Rock climbing in the 1890's.

"At that time comparatively little rock climbing had been done in North Wales. Tryfan was beginning to be recognised as a fairly safe mountain for the beginner and learner . . . The rock faces of the Glyders had never been climbed, nor had Twll Du, commonly known as the Devil's Kitchen . . . In most of the early climbs I had the good fortune to be associated with Archer Thompson, afterwards a member of the Alpine Club, a most excellent all-round mountaineer, especially on rock faces, without whose aid certainly many of the more dangerous climbs would not have been mastered. Another man who was closely connected with us in our climbs was Henry Edwards, then living in Bangor, whose dry humour relieved many a wearing experience. The number therefore as a rule consisted of three, a perfect number for rope work on a difficult climb . . . Our general headquarters were either at Pen-y-Gwryd or at Ogwen Cottage, but sometimes at an out-of-the-way farm house, with an occasional visit further afield or to Cader Idris.

Both Mrs. Owen at Pen-y-Gwryd and Mrs. James at Ogwen always most good-naturedly received and fed us if we turned up, no matter at what hour, even if they had retired for the night. In winter, if we could complete the difficult climb before dark, we were satisfied. We depended on a single folding lantern, lighted by a candle to guide us down. On occasions naturally we got into difficulties . . . There were no motors or buses in our days. We generally finished a days climbing at Llanberis too late for the last train and, after supper at the hotel, walked the ten miles to Bangor. Or, finishing at Pen-y-Gwryd, had dinner there, and started on the 18 or 19 miles walk back to Bangor.

Henry Hughes.

Climbers ascending the Ordinary route on the Idwal Slabs on an unusually quiet day. It was probably opening time! On the left is a climber starting up the first pitch of Tennis Shoe, a delicate climb which as one might expect from its name was first climbed by a leader wearing tennis shoes in 1919 (N.E. Odell).

△ Below the east face of Tryfan.

Snowdon and Y Garn from Penyrole-wen. ▽

△ Below Cader Idris with the Cyfrwy Arete on the left.

Climbing the Cyfrwy Arete, looking down on Llyn y Gaddir. ▽

Llyn Idwal 'on a cloudy afternoon'

George and Ashley Abraham.

The Climber's rig.

The Idwal Slabs.

"Moderately difficult, number immaterial. Leader requires 40′ of rope.

A good and much frequented climb lies up them. A cairn marks the starting-point. A shallow groove, heathery in parts, but furnished with adequate holds is followed for fully 300′. A projection, crowned by a lodged boulder is then close by on the right side. This may be climbed either fairly straight or by a zig zagging edge. An easy alternative lies on the left. From the terraces thus attained the climber can descend to the lower end of Cwm Cneifon, continue upwards by an obvious route to the top of the shoulder, or reach the same by interesting variants above the slabs."

J.M.A. Thompson. 'Climbing in the Ogwen District'. 1910.

The route known as Hope was originally called Minerva 'to mark the fact that it came from feminine skill and prudence,' having been first led by Mrs. Daniell.

It was later re-christened 'Hope' — as it was hoped that the climb could be continued on the steeper cliffs above.

Tennis Shoe was first climbed in 1919 by N.E. Odell who later became a big name in the Himalayas.

The first ascent of the Idwal Slabs by a dog is accredited to Sancho Panza, a spaniel owned by I.A. Richards. 'It was equipped with a chest harness and would gallop up the slabs on a rope.' (Dorothy Pilley).

Exhibitionists!
Just after the First World War Geoffrey Winthrop Young wrote:—
"The Idwal Slabs of our disregard were now, like the Napes Needle providing an ideal theatre for the appraisment of style, and our elder surviving climbers were here joining the younger entry in displaying the new progress."

A decade later.
"On the Idwal Slabs things are getting a trifle congested; there are so many people and so many scratches that it is very difficult to find fresh ground wheron to eat one's sandwiches or leave people one may not want."

J.M. Edwards 1931.

F.E. Hicks was a young Cambridge climber who put up seven new routes on the Idwal Slabs in 1929. C.J. Ashley Cooper described how he accomplished these climbing feats whilst wearing the unlikely climbing garb of Oxford Bags. "It was always a source of wonder to me when watching him climb, how he ever managed to put his feet in the right place, for at each step his foot disappeared into a vast cavern of flannel from which it seemed fated never to reappear."

The Ballad of Idwal Slabs

(To be spoken dramatically in costume: deerstalker hat, side-whiskers, and alpenstock)

"I'll tell you the tale of a climber; a drama of love on the crags;
A story to pluck at your heart-strings, and tear your emotions to rags.
He was tall, he was fair, he was handsome; John Christopher Brown was his name:
The Very Severes nearly bored him to tears — and he felt about girls much the same.

Till one day, while climbing at Ogwen, he fell (just a figure of speech)
For the President's beautiful daughter, named Mary Jane Smith —what a peach!
Her figure was slim as Napes Needle, her lips were as red as Red Wine;
A regular tiger, she'd been up the Eiger North Wales, with no pitons at all!

Now Mary had several suitor's but never a one would she take,
Though it seemed that she favoured one fellow, a villain named Reginald Hake;
This Hake was a Cad who used pitons, and wore a long silken moustarsh,
Which he used, so they say, as an extra belay—but perhaps we are being too harsh.

John took Mary climbing on Lliwedd, and proposed while on Mallory's Slab;
It took him three pitches to do it, for he had'nt much gift of the gab.
He said: "Just belay for a moment—there's a little spike close to your knee—
And tell me, fair maid, when you're properly belayed, would you care to bitch up with me?"

Said Mary. "It's only a toss-up between you and Reginald Hake,
And the man I am going to marry must perform some great deed for my sake.
I will marry whichever bold climber shall excel at the following feat—
To climb headfirst down Hope, with no rubbers or rope,
At our very next climbing-club Meet!"

Now when Mary told the Committee, she had little occasion to plead,
For she was as fair as a jug-handle hold at the top of a hundred-foot lead.
The Club ratified her proposal, and the President had to agree;
He was fond of his daughter, but felt that she oughter
Get married, between you and me.

△ The Rhinogs from the east.

Aran Fawddwy from Craig Cowarch. ▽

△ On Pen Allt-mawr in the Black Mountains.

Brecon Beacons from Pen-y-Crug. ▽

There was quite a big crowd for the contest, lined up at the foot of the Slabs;
The Mobs came from Bangor in Buses, and the Nobs came from Capel in Cabs.
There were Fell and Rock, Climbers', and Rucksack, and the Pinnacle Club (in new hats)
And—sight to remember!—an Alpine Club Member, in very large crampons and spats!

Llyn Idwal, Twll Du and Glyder Fawr. George and Ashley Abraham.

The weather was fine for a wonder; the rocks were as dry as a bone.
Hake arrived with a crowd of his backers, but John Brown strode up quite alone;
A rousing cheer greeted the rivals; a coin was produced, and they tossed.
"Have I won!" cried John Brown as the penny came down.
"No, you fool" hissed his rival. "You've lost!"

So Hake had first go at the contest; he went up by the Ordinary Route,
And only the closest observer would have noticed a bulge in each boot.
Head first he came down the top pitches, applying his moustache as a brake;
He did'nt relax till he'd passed the Twin Cracks, and the crowd shouted, "Attaboy, Hake!"

At the foot of the Slabs Hake stood sneering, and draining a bottle of Scotch;
"Your time was ten seconds," the President said, consulting the Treasurer's watch.
"Now, Brown, if you'd win, you must beat that." Our hero's sang froid was sublime;
He took one look at Mary, and—light as a fairy—ran up to the top of the climb.

Now though Hake had made such good going, John wasn't discouraged a bit,
For that he was the speedier climber even Hake would have had to admit.
So, smiling as though for a snapshot, not a hair of his head out of place,
Our hero John Brown started wriggling down—but look! what a change on his face!

Prepare for a shock, gentle ladies; gentlemen, check the blasphemous word;
For the villainy I am to speak of is such as you never heard!
Reg. Hake had cut holes in the toes of his boots, and filled up each boot with soft soap!

As he slid down the climb, he had covered with slime every handhold and foothold on Hope!

Conceive (if you can) the tense horror that gripped the vast concourse below,
When they saw Mary's lover slip downwards like an arrow that's shot from a bow!
"He's done for!" gasped twenty score voices. "Stand from under!" roared John from above.
As he shot down the slope, he was steering down Hope—still fighting for life and for love!

Like lightning he flew past the Traverse—in a flash he had reached the Twin Cracks—
The friction was something terrific—there was smoke coming out of his slacks—
He bounced on the shelf at the top of Pitch Two, and bounded clean over its edge!
A shout of "He's gone!" came from all—except one; and that one, of course, was our Reg.

But it's not the expected that happens—in this sort of story, at least;
And just as John thought he was finished, he found that his motion had ceased!
His braces (pre-war and elastic) had caught on a small rocky knob,
And so, safe and sound, he came gently to ground 'mid the deafening cheers of the mob!

"Your time was five seconds!" the President cried. "She's yours, my boy—take her! You win!"
"My hero!" breathed Mary, and kissed him; while Hake gulped a bottle of gin,
And tugged his moustache as he whispered, "Aba! my advances you spurn!
Curse a chap that wins races by using his braces!" and he slunk away ne'er to return.

They were wed at the Church of St. Gabbro; and the Vicar, quite carried away,
Did a hand-traverse into his pulpit, and shouted out "Let us belay!"
John put the ring on Mary's finger—a snap-link it was, made of steel,
And they walked to the taxis 'neath an arch of ice-axes, while all the bells started to peal.

The Morals we draw from this story are several, I'm happy to say:
It's Virtue that wins in the long run; long silken moustaches don't pay;
Keep the head uppermost when you're climbing; if you must slither, be on a rope;
Steer clear of the places that sell you cheap braces—and the fellow that uses Soft Soap!"

Showell Styles. 'The Mountaineers' Weekend Book'. 1952.

Holly Tree Wall (above the Idwal Slabs).
"In a very few minutes I.A.R. was writhing among the prickles of a holly-tree.* It was a very robust growth, leaving little or no room to squeeze oneself past between its trunk and the walls of the deep little cleft it grows in. Deep enough for us all three to gather there, though I was left perched amid the worst of the prickles wishing I had on the leather coat I sometimes wear in winter."

Dorothy Pilley. 'Climbing Days'. 1935.

**The holly tree disappeared many years ago.*

The Devil's Staircase (Clogwyn y Geifr).
This route was first ascended in 1898 by O.G. Jones and G.D. Abraham.
"The top pitch 'proved to be a veritable chimney, for a black hole led upwards, apparently into the very heart of the mountain; and we christened the place the Devil's Drainpipe . . . the leader crawled up into its dark recesses, and the sounds of progress gradually faded into the distance, until I heard a call from the open air some fifty feet above my head. At the same time there was an ominous rumble in the Drainpipe! It took a second to realise that a rock was

The Diving Board in the Brecon Beacons.

descending its dark interior, and there seemed every probability that it would sweep me off the small ledge on which I stood. It was a helpless feeling, but the suspense was soon over for the rock whizzed out of the dark hole, and before the real danger could be appreciated, it had scratched some skin off my left ear, and gone crashing down the cliff to the bottom of the gully''.

George and Ashley Abraham. 'Rock Climbing in North Wales'. 1906.

Monolith Crack.
First climbed by the Abraham Brothers in May 1905 (By the outside route).

This climb is more of a caving expedition than anything else; that is if you are thin enough to slide into the notorious crack. It was at one time rated as the hardest climb in North Wales.

Gripping.
''The tenacious way in which the Monolith Crack grips those who enter it minimises the danger of the place, but the difficulties of ascent are such that the writer looks on it as almost the stiffest problem in Wales, and distinctly harder that the famous Kern Knotts Crack in Cumberland.''

George D. Abraham. 'British Mountain Climbs'. 1909.

Do it before breakfast.
''For physical effort the Monolith Crack stands by itself. The amount of exertion required varies approximately as the square of the length of limb between knee and ankle, so some tall men find it quite impossible to get up. Many a defeated opponent has sought to wreak a dastardly revenge by denying that the Monolith has any connection whatsoever with the sport of rock-climbing as properly constituted, while those who succeed are apt to sing its praises somewhat unduly. However, we may confidently assert that the Crack is an excellent training climb, and that by doing it before breakfast much merit may be acquired.''

C.F. Holland 1924.

Climb like a caterpillar.
''I got too much inside the narrow crack and found further progress inpossible. In fact it was a difficult matter to even extricate myself from the vice-like grip . . . As there was little danger of falling out of such a quandry, we neglected the question of anchorage, and my brother mounted into the foot of the crack. It was an easy matter to climb over him and thus effect a splendid lodgement high up in the crack without undue fatigue. . . the upper portion demanded every iota of surplus energy and strength . . . by a series of spasmodic caterpillar-like movements it was possible to make upwards progress.''

G.D. Abraham. 'Rock Climbing in North Wales'. 1905.

The outside variation was climbed by M. de Selincourt in 1923.

Ogwen Cottage.
'' . . . has been a name in the history of mountaineering. It rivalled Pen-y-Gwryd and Pen y Pass in the classic pre-war days, when the art of rock climbing was in course of evolution. It has been kept these fifty years or so by Mrs. Jones, and when last I passed it, Mrs. Jones (who must now be about 86) was standing by the door, not looking a week older than when I first knew her, fifteen years ago.

She is as indominitable as the rugged face of Pen yr Oleu Wen, on which her windows look out, across the foot of Llyn Ogwen. I remember Mr. Jones too, as a man of indominitable spirit; at the age of 70, he bought a Ford car, and learned to drive it, which he found easier than the Saxon tongue.''

Patrick Monkhouse 'On Foot in North Wales'. 1934.

Tryfan.
Tryfan is a three thousand-foot rocky mountain standing at the eastern end of the Glyders above Llyn Ogwen. Its name has been translated variously as the Peak of the Pass or Peak of the Passage. Spelt as Trifaen it is said to mean Three Stones or Three Pointed or Extremely Peaked. According to the 6th century Bard Taliesin, there were once three stones on the summit but now there are only two which are popularly known as Adam and Eve or the shepherd and his wife.

Claim for first ascent in 1867.
'. . . have just made the first ascent of Tryfan. We think it is the most difficult to climb of all the Welsh mountains.'

R.W. Baddeley (Oxford), J.B. Baddeley (Cambridge), Visitors Book at Pen-y-Gwryd 1867.

However it was scaled without difficulty in 1860!
'The sharp cone of Y Tryfan (Three Peaks) rises like the fragment of a great wall seemingly inaccessible, although in reality it may be scaled without much difficulty among the shattered blocks of stone that lie in strange confusion on its steep western side.'

A.C. Ramsay 1860.

And also in 1798!
In 1798, two clergymen, Peter Williams and William Bingley ascended Tryfan from Cwm Bochlwyd. Bingley later claimed that 'they had to use their hands every dozen steps.'

Ascent by the North Gully. (East face of Tryfan).
Tom and Roderick Williams climbed the North Gully on the East Face of Tryfan and are credited with the first roped ascent in Wales.

Stopped by a precipice.
Pennant looked at it from the summit of Glyder Fach and said "It assumes a pyramidal form, naked and rugged . . . A precipice from the summit of which I surveyed the strange scene forbode my approach to examine the nature of its composition."

An arduous and difficult mountain.
"This mountain is in fact a spur, or gigantic 'horn' of the Glyder. The ascent to the summit of Trifaen is both arduous and difficult, and requires considerable nerve, as the mountain on all sides is exceedingly precipitous. Two columnal stones on its peaked summit, similar in formation to those on the Glyder, are frequently mistaken by travellers on the Holyhead road — which runs at the foot of the mountain — for human figures. Some years ago, a gentleman who had ascended Trifaen, performed the hazardous, foolhardly exploit of jumping from one of these stones to the other. If his foot had slipped, or he had lost his balance, he would have been dashed to pieces on the rocks below."

John Henry Cliffe. 'Notes and Recollections of an Angler'. 1860.

A pyramid of beauty.
"I was up Tryfan the other day, that fine rock pyramid over Lake Ogwen, and got on capitally, though it is all regular rock-climbing. Certainly on Tryfan one uses one's feet. There is, I think, no more beautiful creature in the world than this mountain. It will hold its own with anything in Switzerland; I don't mean for difficulty, but for beauty."

Thomas Edward Brown.

Just a large lumpy hill.
All George Borrow had to say about Tryfan was to remark that it was:— "The first of a chain on the left . . . a large lumpy hill with a precipice towards the road probably three hundred feet high." *This precipice that he referred to was probably the Milestone buttress which is now a popular crag for rock climbers who dislike walking and like to climb within spitting distance of their cars.*

Looming above the bonnet of this vintage Rolls Royce is the east face of Tryfan with the Heather Terrace clearly defined. This is a popular ascent route and it also provides an access point for numerous rock climbs of varying grades of difficulty. They all head in the general direction of the summit and provide scope for traditional mountaineering days where one gains the top of a mountain rather than a roadside crag.

A matter of height.

"Tryfan is a mountain of which one becomes extraordinarily fond. It may seem a queer word to use, 'fond' when you see it for the first time — from almost any angle.

I remember walking up the old road from Capel Curig with a friend in the gathering dusk and as we rounded Allt yr Ogof, Tryfan hunched huge black shoulders over us, like a bully with a touch of supernatural in him, and my friend (who had not seen the mountain before) shuddered at it.

There is no way up Tryfan that does not call for the use of the hands, if only for a pull and a touch or two, as well as of the feet. You can come down by the South Ridge, more or less, without using your hands at all, and in my hardy youth I have done it; but it needs smart footwork, and an unashamed use of the elbows, and does not seem, in recollection worth doing. Any other possible route involves a good deal of easy scrambling.

It is a matter for deep thankfulness that the height of Tryfan is 3010′ and not 2990′. Never did mountain strive harder or deserve better, to rank with the Munros."

Patrick Monkhouse. On Foot in North Wales 1934.

Scrambling up the North Ridge of Tryfan is an enjoyable and rewarding experience. The holds are good and height is gained quickly.

Ascent by the North Ridge.

"The North Ridge of Tryfan is a more ambitious and exacting ascent, but it is often done, and is quite safe and easy enough for any able-bodied person. The height to be made from the shore of Llyn Ogwen, is almost exactly 2,000 feet, and the distance less than a mile. But you can spend two hours over it comfortably.

The North Ridge of Tryfan provides a very fine approach to the summit and on the way one encounters a well known and obvious hunk of rock which is generally known as the Cannon. Stand your friend precariously on the end of it and you can take a photograph that never fails to impress. This rock is also referred to as the Crocodile and it is situated at a height of about 1,000′ above Llyn Ogwen.

If you stand near Ogwen Cottage, looking at the North Ridge, you will see, about half way up where the angle steepens, a projecting spike of rock in the likeness of a cannon. This is the point at which to strike the crest of the ridge. But you cannot do it directly; the near west face of the mountain is defended by a continuous rock curtain which, while it offers little resistance to the climber, is not passable without climbing. The obstacle must be outflanked by an excursion on the far side of the ridge. Leave the road at the milestone (the tenth from Bangor) and cut across the big boulders to the foot of the Milestone Buttress, the fine clean mass of rock opposite; then leaving the buttress on the right hand, scramble along under its left wing, and up to the small saddle which is conspicuous from the road. Having thus rounded the buttress, you can turn up to the right, and work towards the crest. It is a wilderness of small rocks, heather and bilberries, but my recollection is that there is a bit of a path to go on with, and presently one emerges at the cannon, which has its emplacement on a patch of level ground. I wouldn't swear to the height, but my guess is that the cannon is about 1000 feet above the lake, that is 2,000 feet above sea-level or a little less.

From this on, follow the steepening crest of the ridge scrupulously. The next 500 feet are fairly easy going. Then the rocks begin, and the way is blazoned with the marks of a thousand nailed boots. Sometimes it wavers a little to the right side of the ridge, then back again; but do not be tempted to diverge to the left, where the angle is much steeper. Archer Thompson says that 'on its crest, wayward humours and lively impulses may be indulged in with impunity'; but this implies to the crest only. About 200 feet from the top, the ridge is interrupted by a conspicuous notch — you can see it from Ogwen — which is circumvented on the right: the North Peak rises from the Notch, and the summit is reached without more ado."

Patrick Monkhouse. 'On Foot in North Wales'. 1934.

Three stones!

"It is the most remarkable rock mountain in Wales; it has two pillar stones on its summit, from which it is often said that the name (= three rocks) is derived. In answer to this it is enough to point out that the assumed stone is not there, and could not have disappeared without a trace; while the name would equally mean 'three peaks' which the mountain certainly has when viewed from east or west. The Welsh dictionaries give a word 'tryfan' with the sense of 'anything spotted through,' and, whether or not this has anything to do with the origin of the name, the component rocks certainly are quartz speckled in a most extraordinary manner."

W.P. Haskett Smith. 'Climbing in the British Isles'. Vol. II 1895.

"The two stones on the top of Tryfan have often been mistaken for men and Mr. Bingley, who made the tour of the country in 1798 and 1801 says:— 'A gentleman of my acquaintance related to me some particulars of his journey, and, among other things told me that, having passed through Nant Francon a little way, he observed on the top of one of the mountains two men that seemed very earnestly engaged in admiring the country. He said that although he went on very slowly, and was constantly looking back at them, till an intervening rock shut them from his sight, yet they still remained in the same position. This story was told so seriously that it was not without difficulty I could keep my countenance to hear it to the end, and, even when I had, I could scarcely persuade him that his men were nothing but blocks of stone.' Bingley was much impressed with the weird grandeur of the place, and it took his breath away to see his companion jumping from one of the stones to the other. None of our readers, let us hope, will be silly enough to repeat a leap that might save them the toil of the descent!"

'Gossiping Guide to Wales'. 1904.

Duty bound.

"The two summit rocks (ten feet high) were to me, as to so many others before and after me, two humans spell-bound in eternal conversation. I was told that they were called Adam and Eve and that a climber's duty was to spring lightly from one to the other."

Dorothy Pilley. 'Climbing Days'. 1935.

Silhouetted against the sky a confident Tryfan man makes the stride from Adam to Eve.

A leaping lady.

''At the very top the climber cannot fail even in mist to recognise the two upright rectangular stones, which are so conspicuous from afar. The feat of jumping from one to the other, by the performance of which Mr. Bingley's friend made that eminent traveller's 'blood chill with horror' nearly a hundred years ago, is not as difficult as it has been represented to be, and the danger of falling over the precipice in case of failure is purely imaginary. The unskilful leaper would merely fall on to the rough stones at the base of the pillars. Of the two jumps, that from north to south is easier. Bingley's guide, perhaps anxious to cap the Saxon's feat, told him that 'a female of an adjoining parish was celebrated for having often performed this daring leap.''

W.P. Haskett Smith. 'Climbing in the British Isles'. Vol. II 1895.

It has become an accepted tradition that in order to claim a true ascent of Tryfan it is necessary to make the famous leap from Adam to Eve. By performing this high level hop you in fact 'receive the freedom of Tryfan'.

R.L.G. Irving in his book 'The Romance of Mountaineering' made the following admission. "It is true that the gap is jumpable, so I have at least one ascent to credit out of some fifty or sixty spurious ones."

I, (the author), remember making my first careful jump to gain my freedom of Tryfan on a misty October afternoon, followed by my companion a few minutes later after some coaxing and cajolong. A lone stranger stood watching us and snorted at our hesitant performance. 'That's easy, you want to try doing press-ups.'

He then climbed confidently onto Adam and stretched across to Eve with his hands on one block and toes on the other. With a large grin on his face he then proceeded to do ten very energetic press-ups. Suddenly his grin vanished and his face went very white. We then heard a frightened voice whisper hoarsely 'Help, I'm stuck, I've run out of strength.' We ambled across and lifted the poor fool down to the rocks below, where he sat with an ashamed look on his face and lit a cigarette with shaking hands.

The Bells! The Bells!

"Standing on the pedestal of Adam, I heard the jangle of Capel Curig bells ringing-in for the eleven o'clock service. A hard frost overnight had made the north ridge tinkle like iron all the way, but now the sun was up bathing the wastes of the Nant Ffrancon in a gentle incandescence. Two thousand feet below, Llyn Ogwen looked near enough for a swallow dive, the A5 road hugging its nearer shore, white as magnesium strip with a flea of a car upon it. Across the valley lay the heaved-up massif of Carnedd — the broad back of Daffyd, with Tryfaen's shadow cast upon it in the shape of a blue wedge, and a spatter of snow on the high table of Llewelyn beyond.

Not so much as a whisper stirred the air, only that muffled chime echoing among the bastions below, sounding for all the world as if the mountain itself were a belfry and the ringers trolls. When at last it ended, the silence dropped like a charm. A charm soon to be broken, for in another hour there would be picknickers hereabouts and a noisy to-do on the crags. For the moment however, the citadel was mine."

W.K. Richmond. 'Climbers Testament'. 1950.

Demon night climbers on the Milestone Buttress.

"I have been to Milestone Buttress on a bewitching summer night, and tried its ascent and descent by aid of an Alpine rope. A Welsh farmer, who suddenly discerned in the gloom a line of men descending like spiders down sheer rocks where, he thought no human foot should tread, departed in haste. The pageant shook forever his sturdy religious denials of witches, orgies and mountain devils. For a year and a day at least he never walked, day or night on Ogwen shore without a comrade or two."

William T. Palmer. 'More Odd Corners in North Wales'. 1946.

Soap Gut.

The story of the first ascent of this unpleasant route is told by Wilfred Noyce in his book 'Mountains and Men.' He was climbing with Menlove Edwards on an April day in 1935.

"Next day it must be something nearer Helyg, for there was no car. 'A cliff near the road,' said Menlove. We attacked Milestone Buttress, fifteen minutes walk up from the Bangor road, at the base of Tryfan. Here are the nail scratches, trade routes that can be seen from miles away on the Carnedds or Elydyr. But again Menlove had an eye for the untrodden rock round the corner; a long groove, this time green and greasy, that splits the buttress frontally. We must traverse into it from the side at half height."

They climbed the today's route of Squint Start to Soap Gut. "Traversing across the Gut, Menlove Edwards jumped for a turf ledge but it collapsed. 'Menlove rose from the depths unmoved, ready to try again.' He announced 'I'm going to jump into the crack. Hold the rope.' He was successful this second time and managed to excavate a good hold. 'The rest was a struggle, muddy in socks up the greasy narrows of the main crack."

They came back the following year to work on their Tryfan guide and on the 4th September they climbed Soap Gut directly from the bottom up the full length of the cleft. Noyce revealed that they found it a 'sticky and frightening struggle,' *and they graded the climb* "very severe, probably about as hard as anything on Tryfan."

On the Milestone Buttress Direct Route. The second man is rounding the awkward corner on the third pitch, where one tries hard not to sit down by maintaining style and balance at the same time.

Munich Climb — Tryfan.
This route was put up by some ace German climbers visiting Wales in 1936. They were taken to the east face of Tryfan by J.R. Jenkins who wrote:— "I had Bellvue Bastion in mind but on reaching the Heather Terrace I remembered an old project of mine to force a route up the wall bounded by the Gashed Crag climb and South Gully. There was a chance that no continuous climb would be found, but I egged on Teufel to try something. A rain-shower delayed operations, but he soon warmed up to it and worked out a route which far exceeded my expectations. It was a very fine lead under the conditions, and provided six excellent pitches, all of a consistently high standard. Two pitons were used."

The route was later climbed by Wilfred Noyce who removed the offending pitons and christened it Munich Climb.

Just for the record.
In 1927 Waller and Palmer made the first ascent of Bell Vue Bastion to the accompaniement of a gramaphone playing on the Bell Vue Terrace below. It was kept going with muscle power and a stock of records provided by a patient colleague.

The Carneddau.

'In spite of the fact that the highest summit is less than 100 feet lower than Snowdon, these great mountains are not popular. They do not advertise their charms; their appearance does not invite; they have no slender pinnacles or gaunt towers to show off to every passer-by, and you may wander many days about them meeting only the wild ponies and the sheep.

Yet the Carnedd ought not to be neglected. The ramble over the ridge from the Sychnant Pass to Ogwen — a dozen miles of moorland and mountain — is one of the finest, and is certainly the highest ridge walk of its kind in Southern Britain. After a mile or two of beautiful going along grassy tracks, one reaches the wet bog, the rough heather and rock of Tal-y-fan where it is good to turn and look back over the broad shoulders of the foothills to the haze of the northern sea, into which the Great Orme is thrown like a clenched fist beyond the sands of Conway. A drop of 600 feet leads to Bwlch-y-Ddeufaen and the Roman road, then up over Drosgl and Drum to the 3,000 foot contour on the walled summit of Foel Fras — a royal road hedged about by the sky and the moors which dip steeply on either side to the long valleys, the sea and the winding silver thread of the river Conway, with the patchwork of field, wood and pasture fading across the whole reach of the Denbigh uplands. Going on over the

The steep south side of Pen yr Ole wen seen from Llyn Idwal.

The name Pen yr Ole wen means Hill of the white light and it is the southern outpost of the Carneddau rising steeply to 3,210 feet above the Ogwen Falls. From its summit is a very fine view to the south directly into Cwm Idwal.

high plateau, Foel Grach is crossed, and then one tackles the last 400 feet of Llewelyn — the mighty chieftain who so long has barred the southward view, till at last the cairn is gained and one greets the faces of friends across the deep trench of Ogwen. Those who are favoured with good conditions will not easily forget the view from the highest Carnedd. Once we were there at sunset upon a July evening, and watched the cliffs of the opposing Glyders and the towers of Tryfan bathe in the magic beauty of a golden air, till the sun sank behind the low cloud-banks in the west — moments of very glorious living which makes up for many disappointments. The true finish to this excursion lies along the rocky ridge to Llewelyn's lesser brother Dafydd, and, seeing the matter through to a rather bitter end, over Pen yr Oleu-wen, down very steep and rough slopes to the outlet of Llyn Ogwen.'

Herbert Carr 'The Mountains of Snowdonia'. 1925.

To the summit of Carnedd Llewelyn. (Second highest mountain in Wales).

"At our feet in a 'yawning abyss' far below, lay the sullen, secluded Llyn Ffynnon Llugwy, the parent of the joyous stream which gladdens the eye of the wanderer as he proceeds to Betwys y Coed.

Here there is socially 'where none intrude' — the shrill whistle of the mountain sheep, the melancholy croak of the solitary raven, or the far-off bark of the shepherd's dog being the only break to the portentuous stillness which reigns; and you are still more deeply impressed 'with the magnitude, the desolation, the intense heart-thrilling solitude' of the lofty mountains you are among. Such were our sensations, as we once more addressed ourselves to the task of accomplishing the crowning object of our excursion — the summit of Carnedd Llewellyn.

The chief labour of the ascent is accomplished on gaining the crest of Bwch Cyfryw Drym; the path hence to the highest point of the mountain is comparatively easy, and we were soon beside the Ordnance carn. We were disappointed to find only very slight traces of Llewelyn's fortified camp from whence he described Bangor in flames, the work of his revengeful father in law, the tyrant John.

A huge carnedd of stones erected by the ordnance surveyors to mark the highest portion of the mountain occupies the site of the camp; and it is probably that during their stay there the entrenchment around the stronghold was in some measure effaced.

It was at this time uncertain whether Snowdon was really the highest mountain in southern Britain; it was affirmed by some authorities that Carnedd Llewelyn was several yards higher; but the recent accurate trignometrical and measurement of the rival monarchs by the officers of the Board of Ordnance puts this 'quaestio vexata' beyond a doubt. The altitude of Carnedd Llewelyn is 3,469′; whilst Snowdon is 3,571′ or something over 100′ higher. Carnedd Dafydd is scarcely inferior to its neighbour being 3,427 feet."

John Henry Cliffe. 'Notes and Recollections of an Angler'. 1860.

The pricely peaks.

"Everybody knows that 'Llewelyn' and 'Dafydd' are the names of Welsh princes, and that the mountains are called after them. But it is probably not true that the eponymous princes were (as most people think) brothers. Welsh mediaeval history records the names of at least five Llewelyns, of whom only one had a brother called Dafydd, and he is not the man after whom the mountain is called. The two best known are Llewelyn ap Iorwerth (known as the Great) who ruled Gwynedd from 1194 to 1240, and was the best prince the Welsh ever had, and Llewelyn ap Gruffyd (known as the last) his grandson, who was finally evicted from his kingdom by Edward I. Carnedd Llewelyn is named after Llewelyn the Great. Llewelyn the Last had a brother, Dafydd and the orthodox view is that Carnedd Dafydd was named after him. But it seems more reasonable to think that it was named after his uncle, Dafydd, son of Llewelyn the Great — much more considerable a person. All these princes lived at Aber, north of the mountain."

Patrick Monkhouse. 'On foot in North Wales'. 1934.

The 14 Peaks Walk.

"Strong walkers will not visit Snowdonia many times without wishing to include the Carnedds, the Glyders and Snowdon in a single expedition. It is a very fine walk and, under favourable conditions well worth doing. In length about 30 miles when taken from Beddgelert or Conway or Llanfairfechan. From thirteen to fourteen hours may be allowed, halts included, at an ordinary pace. It can be greatly reduced by making the Ogwen Valley and Pen-y-Pass the points of departure and arrival. If a part of the walk has to be done in the dark, it is best to reserve the paths of Snowdon for the night watches. A moon, preferably full, is to be desired."

Herbert Carr. 'The Mountains of Snowdonia'. 1925.

Eustace Thomas *was a Manchester engineer who is chiefly remembered for having designed the very successful Thomas stretcher used by Mountain Rescue teams largely unaltered for many years. But Thomas was also the first to traverse the fourteen 3000' summits in North Wales, which is now one of the most popular long distance mountain walks in Britain. In the Alps he became the first man to ascend all the 4,000 metre peaks. This undertaking was done over a six year period and he climbed 83 peaks (over 4,000 metres) which was an average of 19 peaks per year and when he had finished he was near his 60th birthday! He lived to the age of 92 and died in October 1960.*

En route for Carnedd Dafydd across a rock strewn plateau.

Travelling Light.

Jack Haines was one of the record breakers of the endurance marathon over the fourteen 3,000' peaks of Snowdonia in the 1940's. It was a hot day so he wore only shorts and boots. Half way round he discarded the shorts and was later given some clothes by a helper to go through Nant Peris, but he stripped again at Blaen-y-Nant and sent a runner ahead to the top of Snowdon with his trousers. However he arrived before the runner. Several ladies including his wife were waiting for him on the summit. She welcomed him with open arms while the others admired the view of the Lleyn Peninsula.

"As late as 1894 twelve climbs only had been made on all the mountains of Snowdonia and virgin faces met the eye on every side. Lliwedd was then spoken of with bated breath, and the veil of mystery, peculiar to the mountain hung impenetrable over three of its four peaks. The major part of Tryfan remained untrodden and climbers were ignorant of the charms of Dinas Mot and Craig yr Ysfa, as were Ordnance Surveyors of their names. No breach had been made in Braich Du. The sheer slabs of Cyrn Las had lured no previous pilgrim from his path to Clogwyn Person and the faces of the Glyders were untouched.

The ensuing decade in which these crags and others were assaulted will, be looked upon by those who knew it as the Golden Age of Pioneering in Snowdonia.

Craig yr Ysfa from the head of Cwm Eigiau.

George and Ashley Abraham.

The crags of Craig yr Ysfa remained unknown till a relatively recent date, they were discovered accidently in 1900, by three chance deserters from a picnic at Clwyd, who revelled next day in the ascent of the deep cleft that cuts them from base to summit. For a further period of several years the Great Gully remained unvisited by its first explorers, but it has now become widely known, and is rightly regarded as second to none in Britain."

J.M. Archer Thompson. 'Climbing in the Ogwen District'. 1910.

The very exposed Pinnacle Wall on Craig yr Ysfa where the first ascent was made solo by Colin Kirkus.

Colin Kirkus was one of those fortunate climbers who could stand for a long time on small footholds without getting cramp. He developed his own particular way of improving friction by tying elastic bands around his toes.

One of his climbing companions was Alan Hargreaves who observed that "the Climbers' Club people seemed to think that he was a bit mad, and our introduction was on that basis — possibly they thought that I was too — anyway, we were both promptly dubbed 'The Suicide Club,' because our first climb together was Holly Tree Wall in nails on a nice wet day."

Colin Kirkus also had a reputation of having an extraordinary appetite and was sometimes referred to as the "eating machine." *Chantrell summed this up as follows:—*

"Those of us who made regular visits to Helyg will never forget the sight of him sitting at the table on a Sunday evening polishing off everything left uneaten. He might commence with a tin of bully, go on to a large plate of porridge, liberally spread with syrup and butter, and then proceed to clear the table systematically. It was a most impressive spectacle."

During the Second World War Colin Kirkus became a navigator in the R.A.F. and he lost his life in action over Germany.

Moel Siabod.
"Moel Siabod serves as a typical example of a hill that looks as if it were always trying to make up its mind whether or not to call itself a mountain. On three sides it is no better than a moorland sheepwalk: you have to go round by Llyn y Foel to see what the decision is."

W.K. Richmond. 'Climbers Testament'. 1950.

Moel Hebog from the west side of Beddgelert.

Moel Hebog.
"Moel Hebog is Beddgelert's mountain. The usual route leaves the Caernarvon road at Pont Allen, passes the farm of Cwmcloch, bears slightly to the right, and follows a line of cairns up a steep shoulder. The cliffs are kept on the right hand during the final scramble to the summit. Haskett Smith mentions three quarters of an hour as a fit allowance for this 2500 feet of ascent 'when in the pink of condition'; but this is Olympic racing: about two hours will generally be required."

Herbert Carr. 'The Mountains of Snowdonia'. 1925.

A man in the pink of condition!
"Moel Hebog was my first hill. I cycled to the Aberglaslyn Pass, left my cycle at the inn and struck straight up the hillside' . . . 'I was not content to reach the summit by an obvious and easy way, and chose for my route a gully cutting through a belt of cliffs. It was my first mountain, and it had to be climbed in a manner worthy of the occasion. Below the gully was a steep slope of boulders. Up this I scrambled, an ever increasing excitement singing within me. Then the jaws of the gully enclosed me. Damp rocks rose on either hand which seemed almost to breathe coldly upon me.

Up and up I climbed. Then of a sudden, I realised that I was no longer scrambling up a slope of loose boulders; I was on rocks — a part of the living mountain. I paused and looked up.

Above me the gully walls, sternly separate, vanished into the mist; the bed of the gully between them was dreadfully steep. I looked down. The portion of the gully I had already climbed looked even steeper, and the initial slope of boulders was far below and remote. All I could see was a narrow vertical slit of hillside veiled with rain.

I was afraid, quite suddenly I was afraid; an empty tingling, an animalish, primitive feeling, not a product of reasoned thought, but a wholly illogical displacement of mental vertebrae. Supposing I slipped? I could imagine the slip: the frantic clutchings, the slide, the sudden bound outwards and downwards, the sickening impact with one wall, then with the other wall of the gully. I saw my body, broken and torn, strike the slope of boulders up which I had scrambled so happily, then roll over and over down it in a loose uncontrolled ridiculous way like a tailor's dummy; half stop, roll on and finally flop to a standstill and sprawl limply and without movement, with glazing eyes — life's hopes and aspirations lost and won in the adventure and mystery of death.

I retreated and during my retreat found that the rocks I had climbed with never a thought of difficulty or danger now seemed both difficult and dangerous, perhaps because they had become wet with rain. I had to curb a tendency to clutch wildly at anything. It was of course an absurdly easy gully. Any rock climber who knows Moel Hebog will marvel at this description but it is a true and unvarnished account of a boy's adventures and impressions. I eventually reached the summit by another route."

F.S. Smythe. 'The Spirit of the Hills'. 1935.

Mynydd Mawr, otherwise known as Elephant Mountain as seen from the Llanberis Path on Snowdon, just above Llyn Du'r Arddu.

Mynydd Mawr.
"Mynydd Mawr rises in lordly isolation, and is a quaintly constructed mountain; seen from the southern slopes of Snowdon its profile resembles an elephant, a fact which provides a popular nickname for the peak."

Herbert Carr. 'The Mountains of Snowdonia'. 1925.

"It (Mynydd Mawr) is made of a very rare intrusive rock called 'riebeckite' — a granite with an overdose of horn-blende and soda. The only other places in the British Isles in which it occurs are Ailsa Caraig, off the Clyde; Rockall out in the Atlantic (If that can be reckoned British Isles); and I believe The Eildon Hills near Melrose. Certainly these crags look like nothing else on earth; a wild array of 'tottering spearheads,' rusty in colour, with long pale screes."

Patrick Monkhouse. 'On Foot in North Wales'. 1934.

Cnicht viewed from the south west on the A487 below Croesor.

Cnicht.
This shapely peak to the south east of Beddgelert is often referred to as the Welsh Matterhorn and George Borrow even went so far as to call it "the conical peak impaling heaven."

In 1857 John Henry Cliffe, the mountaineering angler ascended Cnicht on September 4th and declared that he had only heard of one other man who had been to the summit before him and that was the "climbing clergyman."

A daring, fatiguing and arduous feat in 1860.

"It is not too much to assert that there is no mountain in Wales — not even Snowdon — that presents to the eye such elegance of outline as the conical summit of Cnicht.

'We were seized with the desire of ascending to the summit of Cnicht; this exploit we know from the appearance of the mountain, would be attended with some difficulty and arduous climbing; but nothing daunted and having recently performed the feat of ascending Moel Hebog unaided and alone, we determined to carry out our purpose on the first fitting opportunity. Few Englishmen have ever stood on the summit of Cnicht; we never met with but one individual who had performed the feat, and this was a clergyman, a perfect enthusiast in mountain scenery — a most intellectual companion.

After a gradual ascent of one hour we approached the plateau, from which rises the cone of Cnicht; and here the real labour of the ascent commenced. On our approach to the foot of the cone, we saw at once that our anticipations of the difficulty of ascending, or rather climbing to the summit, were not magnified. Path there was none; the steep incline was covered with small loose debris, and on the south side, looking down into Cwm Croesor, the mountain was a sheer precipice, absolutely inaccessible. It was some little time before we could summon up courage to commence our task; and it was not until after several repulses, from the difficulty of keeping our footing that we succeeded in accomplishing the ascent.

We at last stood upon the summit of the cone. Here the Ordnance Surveyors have created a carnedd; and being exposed to the wind, which began to blow freshly, we were glad to repose under its lee. We had no conception that the view would have been so extensive or so magnificent, and it was sometime before we could take in all the details of the splendid panarama around us . . .

After spending more than an hour in the silent contemplation of these splendid works of nature we reluctantly began to retrace our steps, which we found almost more arduous and fatiguing than the ascent."

John Henry Cliffe. 'Notes and Recollections of an Angler'. 1860.

Feel them ye feet,
The spring of heather and the shrinking snow.
Cloud and the dews of night
Leave them for your delight,
That ye may gladly go
Through the grim city and the cobbled street:
Feel them for hope, light feet.

Hold them ye hands,
The rough granite and the stinging rain.
Earth stores them on hill-slope,
Cleansing and clasp of hope.
To cheer your age again
Groping in darkness through the last grey lands:
Hold them for strength, sure hands.

Take them, O heart
The joy of comrades and the thrill of strife
Who has the hills for friend
Has a God-speed to end
His path of lonely life,
And wings of golden memory to depart:
Take them for love, true heart."

Geoffrey Winthrop Young 'Wind and Hill'. 1909.

The Moelwyns from Blaenau Ffestiniog.

The Moelwyns.

"The two Moelwyns suffer from remoteness: the nearest village is Ffestiniog, in the slate area, but an ascent from Beddgelert is fairly easy, a well marked path crossing between the two hummocks at somewhere near 2,000 feet above the sea."

W.T. Palmer. 'The Splendour of Wales'. 1932.

Yr Eifli (known in English as The Rivals).

"We were only able to find time for the ascent of the central peak of the Rivals, which is surrounded by a stupendous mass of debris, and forms as wild a scene as can well be imagined. The Ordnance Surveyors have erected a lofty wooden post in a heap of stones on the summit. The post is covered with inscriptions and the initials of numerous visitors. This custom is a habit belonging exclusively to the English. How frequently we see the most handsome monuments disfigured by this vulgar and barbarous practice.

The Rivals are said to abound in magnetic-iron stone, and it is generally believed by sailors that when ships approach them, the compass becomes much affected. We have ourselves observed a curious phenomenon whilst in the neighbourhood of these mountains. In the finest weather, when not a cloud or vapour was discernable in any direction, small ragged spots or lumps of vapour would suddenly form, and rapidly drift along the sides of the mountain and then almost as quickly disappear.

The Yr Eifli range, although not lofty, assume a bold appearance, from their proximity to the sea; dividing, as it were, the generally flat dreary Peninsula of Lleyn from the flat marsh coast of Clynnog and Caernarvon. Their graceful outline and picturesque appearance render them amongst the most attractive features of Caernarvonshire: but they are rarely visited by tourists, being out off the beaten path, and the Peninsula of Lleyn is almost a term incognito.

A ramble into that wild primitive country, however is very enjoyable; its antiquarian treasures are of the highest interest: and a pilgrimage to Bardsey Isle, an event never to be forgotten."
John Henry Cliffe. 'Notes and Recollections of an Angler'. 1860.

The central summit of Yr Eifl on the Lleyn Peninsula.

Rhinog Fawr.
"It is one of the barest and most rocky mountains in all Wales, and yet it has hardly anywhere on it a crag of respectable height. Little nameless problems, however, abound, and men who are content to enjoy a day's promiscuous scrambling, without accomplishing any notorious climb about which they will afterwards be able to boast may be recommended to ramble over Rhinog Fawr."
W.P. Haskett Smith. 'Climbing in the British Isles'. Vol. II 1895.

Ravenous on the Rhinogs.
"There was a day on the Rhinogs when, for the first time in my life the phrase 'weary unto death' became more than a figure of speech. Seven hours without bite or sup, and the way back to Tyn y Groes lay over miles of bogland. Rummaging round in my rucksack, all I could find was an inch or so of mouldy crust, relic of a month old packed lunch. Still, beggars could not be choosers. To keep body and soul together, I munched it mould and all. The effect was instantaneous: if it had been brandy it could not have been more reviving. Like Absalom after he had tasted honey, my eyes were enlightened. The air itself assumed an aura of wonder. The moor glowed, all its moss cushions bright in emerald and gold, every blade of rush-grass-a-twinkle. I went on my way singing."
W.K. Richmond. 'Climber's Testament'. 1950.

"My first visit to the Rhinogs was many years ago in the company of a maiden aunt. We made no attempt to reach the summits, but did the round of the Roman Steps and the Pass of

Ardudwy. We drove to the farm of Dolwreiddiog, a mile short of Llyn Cwm Bychan, and walked the rest of the round. The aunt walked very well, but when we emerged from Bwlch y Tyddiad, and after proceeding a short distance along the Trawsfynnydd path, started to walk across the moor to the path which goes through the Pass of Ardudwy, she was exceedingly indignant because the moor was very boggy. I believe she thought it great remissness on the part of the 'Authorities' (whoever they might be). She had a most elegant umbrella with her, and when it sank into the peat bog for about half its length, and smirched its maiden purity, she was very wroth. Vain, of course, to tell her that she ought not to have brought an umbrella at all. The feminine mind clings to an umbrella as a sheet-anchor, whether it is for a tramp over the mountains where of course it is utterly useless, or whether it be for a walk down Regent Street."

Arthur L. Bagley. 'Holiday Rambles in North Wales.' 1925.

The distinctive skyline of the Rhinog range viewed from the east.

Tom the tourist.

"Here lies the body of poor Tom Best
Who climbed the mountain in Summer vest,
Who loved the lonely hills to roam,
But he left his map and compass at home!!
He lived a blameless life, 'tis clear,
But he certainly wasn't a mountaineer!!"

Anon.

The so called 'Roman Steps' which ascend Bwlch Tyddiad from Cwm Bychan.

The Roman Steps.

"Up through a narrow cut in this mountain wall climbs that long, mysterious stone stairway known as the 'Roman Steps'. There must be several hundred of them, some sections more perfect than others, laid obviously by hand and extending for perhaps half a mile."

A.G. Bradley 'In Praise of North Wales'. 1925.

The Arenigs.

"Inland it is the dome of Arenig Fawr (2,800′) which infalliby draws the eye, a sturdy, well-set-up figure of a mountain, all the more splendid for its isolation. Look it out on the map and you will see how it is ringed around with ranges on all sides, except on the N.E. On a clear day all the main groups of North and Central Wales are visible from it; and the profiles of Snowdonia, set out in echelon as seen across the sodden wastes of Migneint, take on a sharper definition. For comprehensiveness and serried beauty, there is no panorama in Wales to equal that from the Arenig cairn, now dedicated as a war memorial to the crew of a Flying Fortress which crashed near the summit."

W. Richmond 'Climbers Testament'. 1950.

"The great mountain of Arenig Fawr rises here abruptly and imposingly to the skies, its rock-fronted crown touching an altitude of 2,800 feet. Tonight it looked merely stern and sombre. Steep as it is I found my way to the top I remember, on a glorious summer evening without any difficulty, though not being climbed by tourists there was no trail. As the king of all the mountains south of Snowdonia and east of Cader and the Arans, it overlooks nearly all North Wales, while as I have already noted, it is often taken for Snowdon from a distance, far away from Snowdon though it be, and 700 feet lower. Then the view from it includes Bala Lake, its long trail mirrored in the middle distance. Under its shadow, too is, Llyn Arenig, a roundish tarn of about a mile in circumference, lapping the base of the almost precipitous south-eastern shoulder of the mountain, which looks imposing from the lake's farther shores.

But a Welsh tarn can be frightfully gruesome on occasions as when a mountain mist descends upon your solitude, and fleecy clouds curl over its black waters and wave their lace like veils against the gloomy precipices that overhang so many of these high tarns in Wales.''

A.G. Bradley. 'In Praise of North Wales'. 1925.

Borrow was impressed.
''Arenig (Fawr) is certainly barren enough, for there is neither tree nor shrub upon it, but there is something majestic in its huge bulk. Of all the hills which I saw in Wales none made a greater impression upon me.''

George Borrow, 'Wild Wales'. 1854.

The fifth summit of Wales.
''Arenig Fawr (2,800′) is called 'Rennig' by Daines Barrington, who writing in 1771, adds that it is commonly considered as the fifth mountain of North Wales in point of height. It was one of our earliest meterological stations, as it was here that the Hon. Daines Barrington conducted his experiments on rainfall in 1771.''

W.P. Haskett Smith. 'Climbing in the British Isles'. Vol. II 1895.

Designed by an architect!
''Arenig (2,800′) is a first-class mountain. It is sculptured from layer on layer of volcanic ash, and its massive limbs are cunningly disposed, as an architect would dispose them, to lead to the final cone, with a sense of deliberate climax.''

Patrick Monkhouse. 'On Foot in North Wales'. 1934.

Arenig Fach approached from the marshy wastes of Migneint.

The heart of North Wales.
''The true heart of North Wales is, by a happy chance, heart shaped. If you take the three chief mountains of this central group, Arenig Fawr, Rhobell Fawr, and the Rhinog range, you can, with a little imagination, produce a colourable imitation of the ace of hearts.''

Patrick Monkhouse. 'On Foot in North Wales'. 1934.

Cader Idris.

It is claimed that Cader Idris is the most popular mountain after Snowdon and the first written record of an ascent seems to have been in 1768. An account of the adventure being published in the 'Gentlemens' Magazine' (Vol XXXVIII p.147).

The highest mountain in Britain?

"Here among innumerable summits, and rising peaks of nameless hills, we saw Kader-Idricks, which some are of opinion, is the highest mountain in Britain, another called Rarauvawr (Yr Aran Fawr), another called Mowylwynda (Moelwyn) and still every hill we saw, we thought was higher than all that ever we saw before."

Daniel Defoe.

"It is a mistake to think that Cader Idris is the second highest mountain in Wales, for there are several other peaks which excel it; nevertheless, it may fairly claim to come next after Snowdon in importance and popularity. Its height is only 2,927 feet, but as it rises almost straight out of the sea it gives the impression of being very much taller. The mountain lacks the exquisitively shaped cone-like summit which so easily wins for Snowdon the place of the most beautiful mountain in England and Wales. The summit of Cader is a blunt ridge. Beneath the highest ridge are other ridges, one below the other, growing broader and broader until the level of the sea is reached. Looked at from Barmouth, the mountain resembles a gigantic staircase, the first landing being the imposing and almost vertical cliffs of Tyrrau Mawr. Many a visitor to the coast has mistaken Tyrrau Mawr for Cader itself, for the latter is apt to hide itself in cloud, and sometimes for days at a time to refuse to allow even a fleeting glimpse of itself. Cader is an exhaustibly varied mountain, in that respect even surpassing Snowdon itself. To know it properly it must be viewed from many points, some of them as much as twenty miles apart. No one has seen it at its best who has not stood on the hill behind Barmouth, while the fading light of an April evening slowly dies upon the cliffs of its western face, and on a morning in winter when its snowy crown glitters in the sunshine."

W. Watkin Davies. 'A Wayfarer in Wales'. 1930.

Four ways to the top.

"There are four logical ways of attacking a range like that of Cader — you may begin at either end, and walk the length of it, glorying all the way in the wind and the prospect over the kingdoms of the earth. Or you may take up the challenge of the mountain and go straight for its peak, where it is highest and steepest, from north or south, like a wolf flying at a man's throat."

Patrick Monkhouse. 'On Foot in North Wales'. 1934.

Cader Idris.

"Last Autumn, as we sat, ere fall of night,
Over against old Cader's rugged face,
We marked the sunset from its secret place
Salute him with a fair and sudden light.
Flame-hued he rose, and vast without a speck
Of life upon his flush'd and lonely side:
A double rainbow o'er him bent, to deck
What was so bright before, thrice glorified!
How oft, when pacing o'er these inland plains,
I see that rosy rock of Northern Wales
Come up before me! then its lustre wanes,
And all the frith and intermediate vales
Are darkened, while our little group remains
Half-glad, half-tearful, as the vision pales!"

Charles Tennyson Turner.

Looking towards Penygadair from Twr Du.

An ascent of Cader Idris.

"We at length approached a dark beetling rock, of shaggy aspect and tremendous height, which stands entirely detached from the neighbouring cliff. Its real name is Craig-Cay; but our guide with pardonable vanity had christened it after himself, and assured us that it was called Pughe's Pinnacle. . . Arriving at the extremity of the pool, we began to ascend the western summit of Cader Idris, a task not only of labour, but of some peril, also it being a different route from that which travellers usually persue: 600′ of steep rock, covered indeed with short grass, but so slippery as to render the footing very insecure. As we approached the top, the ascent became more abrupt, whilst the scene below us, of craggy rocks, perpendicular precipices, and an unfathomable lake, did not operate to lessen the alarm that a person unaccustomed to so dangerous a situation naturally feels. Our companion the mountaineer, skipped on the meanwhile with the agility of a goat, and whilst we were dumb with terror, descanted on the beauties of Cader Idris and the excellence of its mutton . . . At length, after excessive labour and repeated efforts, we gained the top of this noble mountain, and were at once recompensed for all the fatigue and alarm of the ascent. The afternoon was gloriously fine, and the atmosphere perfectly clear, so that the vast unbounded prospect lay beneath us, unobscured by cloud, vapour or any other interruption to the astonished and delighted eye, which threw its glance over a varied scene, including a circumference of at least 500 miles. To the north-west is seen Ireland, like a distant mist upon the ocean; and a little to the right, Snowdon, and the other mountains of Caernarvonshire. Further on in the same direction, the Isle of Man, the neighbourhood of Chester, Wrexham, and Salop; the sharp head of the Wrekin, and the undulating summit of the Clee hills. To the south we have the country round Clifton, Pembrokeshire, St. Davids, and Swansea; and to the westward a vast prospect of the British Channel unfolds itself, which is bounded only by the horizon."

Richard Warner.

The present day shelter near the summit of Penygadair — a dark and dismal place to eat your sandwiches. It is usually so full of litter, dank and smelly that most people prefer to sit outside in the rain.

The summit cairn of Penygadair.

Sleeping on Cader Idris.
According to popular legend — he who sleeps in the chair of Idris on the summit of the mountain will be found the next morning, a corpse, a madman or a bard. The result of a night spent on Snowdon is very much the same. (see page 23).

An instant poet!

"I lay there in silence — a spirit came o'er me —
Man's tongue hath no language to speak what I saw!
Things glorious, unearthly, passed floating before me,
And my heart almost fainted with rapture and awe!
I viewed the dread beings around us that hover
Though veiled by the mists of mortality's breath;
I called upon darkness the vision to cover
For a strife was within me of madness and death."

Mrs. Heman.

The mad folk down below.
"On the top of Cader Idris I felt how happy a man might be with a little money and a sane intellect, and reflected with astonishment and pity on the madness of the multitude."

T.L. Peacock.

On the summit in 1840.
"Here we became enveloped in vapour which continued to boil and curl around us during the whole of the time we remained on the summit, with the exception of a few brief intervals. We visited Pugh's hut, what he called his 'hotel' a rudely built pile of stones, but it was so damp

and dark in the interior, that we were glad to exchange our quarters for the lee of the huge carnedd, or mound of stones erected by the Ordnance Surveyors."

John Henry Cliffe June 20th 1840.

Photo — George and Ashley Abraham

Llyn Cau on the south side of Cader Idris — a dramatic and beautiful location.

"Cader has something for everybody, from the wall-of-death exponent on Cyfrw to the school-marm in charge of a troop of Brownies. Without the assistance of a rack and pinnion Railway, it draws the multitudes as no other summit in Britain does and still manages to preserve itself unsullied; a walker's mountain first and foremost possibly, but indubitably a mountain. Its walls may not be three miles high, as they were once reputed to be, but they are three miles long, uncompromisingly precipitous most of the way, and quite the next-best-thing to the Glyders by being grandly scarped on their southern side as well. The ascent from Tal y Llyn, wooded at first, then opening out into the ampitheatre hollow beneath Craig y Cau, is as magnificent as any in the Principality."

W. Kenneth Richmond 'Climbers Testament'. 1950.

Only a hill but . . .

"Only a hill: yes looked at from below:
Facing the usual sea, the frequent west.
Tighten the muscle, feel the strong blood flow,
And set your foot upon the utmost crest!
There where the realms of thought and effort cease,
Wakes on your heart a world of dreams and peace."

Geoffrey Winthrop Young.

The Difficult Pitch in the Great Gully, Craig y Cae. George and Ashley Abraham.

The Cyfrwy arete.

"Away to the right is a bold crag, Cyfrwy which played a not important part in mountaineering history, for in 1909, Mr. Arnold Lunn fell off it and broke his leg. The leg mended, but he had to give up rockclimbing and to concentrate his powers on skiing; and since he has done more than any man to make skiing an essential subject in the curriculum of the whole mountaineer."

Patrick Monkhouse. 'On Foot in North Wales'. 1934.

The Cyfrwy Arete on the north side of Cader Idris.

A distinctive feature on this route is 'The Table'.

A Loose Rock

The day was perfect. The burnished silver of the sea melted into a golden haze. Light shadows cast by scudding clouds drifted across the blue and distant hills. The sun flooded down on the rocks. I slid down the crack and reached the top of the steep face of rock above 'The Table' The usual route dodges the top fifteen feet of this face, and by an easy traverse reaches a lower ledge. But on that glorious afternoon I longed to spin out the joys of Cyfrwy, and I found a direct route from the top to the bottom of this wall, a steep but not very severe variation.

It was one of those days when to be alive is 'very heaven.' The feel of the warm, dry rocks and the easy rhythm of the descending motion gave me an almost sensuous pleasure. One toyed with the thought of danger, so complete was the confidence inspired by the firm touch of the wrinkled rocks.

In this short span
Between my finger tips and the smooth edge,
And these tense feet cramped to a crystal ledge,
I hold the life of man.

Consciously I embrace,
Arched from the mountain rock on which I stand
To the firm limit of my lifted hand.
The front of time and space;

For what is there in all the world for me
But what I know and see?
And what remains of all I see and know
If I let go?

I was glad to be alone. I revelled in the freedom from the restraints of the rope, and from the need to synchronize my movements with the movements of companions.

I have never enjoyed rock-climbing more. I have never enjoyed rock-climbing since. But, at least, the hills gave me of their best, full measure and overflowing, in those last few golden moments before I fell.

A few minutes later Lindsay, who was admiring the view from Cader, was startled by the thunder of a stone avalanche. He turned to a stray tourist, urging him to follow, and dashed off in the direction of Cwfrwy.

And this is what had happened. I had just lowered myself off the edge of 'The Table' — conspicuous in Mr. Abraham's excellent photograph. There was no suggestion of danger. Suddenly the mountain seemed to sway, and a quiver ran through the rocks. I clung for one brief moment of agony to the face of the cliff. And then suddenly a vast block, which must have been about ten feet high and several feet thick, separated itself from the face, heeled over on top of me, and carried me with it into space. I turned a somersault, struck the cliff some distance below, bounded off once again and, after crashing against the ridge two or three times, landed on a sloping ledge about seven feet broad. The thunder of the rocks falling through the hundred and fifty feet below my resting-point showed how narrow had been my escape.

I had fallen a distance which Lindsay estimated at a hundred feet. It was not a sliding fall, for except when I struck and rebounded I was not in contact with the ridge. The fall was long enough for me to retain a very vivid memory of the thoughts which chased each other through my brain during those few crowded seconds. I can still feel the clammy horror of the moment when the solid mountain face trembled below me, but the fall, once I was fairly off, blunted the edge of fear. My emotions were subdued, as if I had been partially anaesthetized. I remember vividly seeing the mountains upside down after my first somersault. I remember the

The Eastern Arete of Cyfrwy from 'The Table'.

George and Ashley Abraham.

disappointment as I realized that I had not stopped and that I was still falling. I remember making despairing movements with my hands in a futile attempt to check my downward progress.

The chief impression was a queer feeling that the stable order of nature had been overturned. The tranquil and immobile hills had been startled into a mood of furious and malignant activity, like a dangerous dog roused from a peaceful nap by some in-attentative passer-by who has trodden on him unawares. And every time I struck the cliff only to be hurled downwards once again, I felt like a small boy who is being knocked about by a persistent bully — 'Will he never stop? . . . surely he can't hit me again . . . surely he's hurt me enough.'

When at last I landed, I tried to sit up, but fell back hurriedly on seeing my leg. The lower part was bent almost at right angles. It was not merely broken, it was shattered and crushed.

I shouted and shouted and heard no reply. Had Lindsay returned home? Would I have to wait for hours before help came?

Solitude had lost its charm. I no longer rejoiced in my freedom from intrusion. On the contrary, I raised my voice and called upon society to come to my assistance. I set immense store on my membership of the Human Club, and very urgently did I summon my fellow-members to my assistance.

And then suddenly I heard an answering cry, and my shouts died away in a sob of heartfelt relief.

And while I waited for help, I looked up at the scar on the cliff where the crag had broken away, and I realized all that I was in danger of losing. Had I climbed my last mountain?"

Arnold Lunn. 'The Mountains of Youth'. 1909.

Pugh — the local guide.
". . . an eccentric character named David Pughe, who acted as guide to the 'sublime mountain Cader Idris,' and seems to have been highly diverted with his pompous manner and affected dignity."

John Henry Cliffe 1840.

His son, Robert Pugh once ascended Cader Idris four times in one day starting and finishing at the Golden Lion Hotel. He won a wager of £10 from a party of gentlemen staying at the hotel and no doubt increased his reputation at the same time. The total distance of 48 miles of ascent and descent was walked in just over twelve hours.

Robert Pugh used to advertise his services as follows:—

"Within a morning's ride, Robert Pugh, denominated 'Guide General' will conduct on (safe and sturdy) ponies the visitors to the waterfalls of Rhaiadr Mawddach and Pistyll y Cain; the first issuing from an elevation of from 50 to 60 feet: and the latter rushing down a vast rock at least 150 feet high.

He will likewise conduct the visitor to Drws Ardudwy and Cymbychan where may be seen a curious specimen of human industry and ingenuity (supposed of Roman origin) in the construction of regularly graduated steps, extending to the amazing distance of two miles commanding the most varied and picturesque scenery. The Torrent's Walk, near Caernwch, and the Precipice Walk, near Nannau, are also well worth visiting, and are admired by all who have seen them, for their unique grandeur.

The Guide General (Robert Pugh) has a cottage on the summit of Cader Idris, where shelter may be had for those who wish to see the rising sun from that elevation; or in case of a shower or any atmospheric, the visitor will find here a shelter on the highest pinnacle of this justly celebrated mountain.

The Arans.
"The Merionethshire Arans are real mountains, not grassy and rounded hills. Feldberg for example is much higher; but when standing on its broad summit you might easily suppose yourself to be on Leith Hill, or even on the downs above Weymouth. Not so, however on the Arans. On the east side, particularly, are precipitous black rocks, which the novice in the art of mountaineering would be well advised to avoid unless accompanied by an experienced guide; but the seasoned cragsman will find on them exhilarating and perfectly safe sport.

The two Arans may be ascended either from the village of Llanuwchllyn in the north, or from Dinas Mawddwy in the south. Personally I prefer the former route; for by it you ascend terrace after terrace, following the ridge which seems to run like a spinal cord from the foot of the mountain to its summit. I always like to think of a mountain as alive, as a friend with whom I am out to spend the day. I hate all short cuts to the summit. I prefer to follow its natural rises step after step until the highest pinnacle is reached. This may not be the best way to tackle the Alps; but then we are speaking of the friendly hills of Wales, not of majestic peaks so far aloof that any thought of friendship with them would savour of impertinence!

By whatever route it is reached, the summit of the Aran is well worth reaching, for it is one of the finest view-points in the whole of Wales. As every mountaineer knows, it is not mere height that guarantees wide prospects: the all important condition is that our mountain should stand well apart from other mountains of approximately equal altitude. This is the case with the Aran. It is consequently well worth while to choose a day when visibility is good. There are many such days in May, June and September. What the wayfarer in Wales should learn as early as possible, and never afterwards forget, is that July and August, generally speaking, are not desirable months for a holiday in the Principality — except of course, for those queer folk who are content to go about in closed motor cars, sallying forth now and again to view one of the more easily reached 'sights Granted a clear day, the panorama beheld from the Aran is extraordinarily fine and extensive. There are no high mountains in the immediate vicinity to cut off the view, as is so often the case in the Snowdonia group of giants; and there is no better platform from which to behold in all their majesty the slopes of the Berwyns, Cader Idris, Plynlimmon, Arenig and the greater peaks of Caernarvonshire."

W. Watkin Davies. 'A Wayfarer in Wales'. 1930.

Aran Benllyn.
"On this mountain is the reputed grave of Rhita Gawr, a giant who lived on Snowdon and had the presumption to demand the beard of King Arthur to place upon the robe he wore, which was adorned by the beards of many other kings whom he had slain or conquered. Rhita felt confident that he could overpower even a mighty warrior like Arthur, but he was wrong. The king refused to part with his beard, whereon Rhitta scornfully challenged him to fight. A mighty combat ensued among the Arans, whose wild scenery seems a fitting background for giants, the rocks shattered as if in Homeric contest. Arthur was victorious, killing Rhitta and burying him on Aran Benllyn."

Hope Hewett. 'Walking through Merioneth'.

Please note that access on the Arans is restricted to a courtesy path across the highest summits by agreement with the landowners.

Aran Mawddwy.
"This is the highest mountain in the county of Merioneth, being 41′ higher than Cader Idris. It is a stiff pull to the summit, but the view from it is very extensive, and under proper lights, magnificent in the extreme."

John Henry Cliffe. 'Notes and Recollections of an Angler'. 1860.

A pointless exercise.
"On the summit of Aran Mawddwy (2,970′) is a huge cairn said to have been erected by the men of Dinas Mawddwy. They heard that the summit of Cader Idris was higher by six

feet and were annoyed that the grandeur of their own mountain should be surpassed. With infinite toil they built the cairn to elevate the crest to seven feet, but it has since been discovered that their efforts were unnecessary as Aran is over forty feet higher even without the cairn!"

Hope Hewett. 'Walking through Merioneth'.

The splendid hut of Bryn Hafod in Cwm Cowarch below the cliffs of Craig Cywarch. It is owned by the Mountain Club of Stafford and was constructed by the club members.

The Berwyns.

"The pedestrian will find the Berwyns a fascinating region to wander in. He might start from Corwen, cross several interesting ridges to the lonely Lake Vyrnwy, then follow a good road to Dinas Mawddwy, and so back to civilisation again at either Machnynlleth or Dolgelley."

W. Watkin Davies. 'A Wayfarer in Wales'. 1930._

Thirst Quencher.

"We walked over the mountains to Bala — most sublimely horrible! It was scorchingly hot. I applied my mouth ever and anon to the side of the rocks and sucked in draughts of water cold as ice, and clear as infant diamonds in their embryo dear."

Coleridge.

The Lost World of the Berwyns.

"The mist got thicker still, and I could now see nothing at all more than a yard or two away, and had to keep looking at the compass continually. In a mist like this one has no sense of size,

Pistyll Rhaeadr at the end of the Rhaeadr valley on the south side of the Berwyns. This is the highest waterfall in Wales with the cascade falling a total height of 100 metres.

and things are distorted and magnified beyond what anybody would believe who had not seen it. For instance, there loomed up through the mist a terrible horned creature, looking gigantic, that stood and surveyed me malevolently. Visions of Conan Doyle's prehistoric monsters came into my mind; had I stumbled upon an enclave in the Berwyns, where dinosaurs and peterodactyls and other fearsome monstrosities still flourished? I could not be 'seeing things,' for it was still early, and no drop of alcoholic refreshment had passed my lips this day, and only one little teeny-weeniest spotlet the night before. Then a familiar 'Baa-a-a' broke the spell: it was but a harmless specimen of genus ovis after all."

Arthur L. Bagley, 'Holiday Rambles in North Wales'. 1925.

The Berwyns.
"The Berwyns (Moel Sych, 2,713′) continue the line begun by Cader and the Arans in nothing like the same vein of high seriousness. Round-shouldered, they look like overgrown downs or, more appropriately like left-overs from the Pennines which have somehow got misplaced. The gradients are gentle enough but what with the heather and the tussocky grass the going is so infernally uneven that it is a case of one foot up and one down from start to finish. Once you are on them, the Berwyns never let go of you for an instant, as if their sole vocation were to knock you and your town-legs into shape or know the reason why."

W.K. Richmond. 'Climbers' Testament'. 1950.

The lower slopes of Plynlimon (Pumlumon Fawr) at Eisteddfa Gurig which is the starting point of the normal ascent route. There is a car park and a cafe here.

Plynlimon — 'the most dangerous mountain in Wales!'
"With respect to Plynillimon mountain, it is either the second or third in Wales, in point of size and height. We may indeed compare it with those formidable personages of poetical creation, who walk with their feet upon the earth, and their heads in the region of the heavens.

Its foot is here in Cardiganshire, but its bald and weather beaten head is at the distance of several miles in Montgomeryshire. I know not, whether, according to the ancient division, it might not have spurned the limits of a single kingdom, yet after all, it is more properly to be considered as a vast bed of mountains, piled one upon another: Alps upon Alps, Pelion upon Offa, or any other magnificent image which the reader may incline to affect. But the ruggedness and inhospitality of its environs is in general so unrelieved, that it affords little food for the picturesque enthusiasm of those who venture on the labours and perils of the ascent. It is the most dangerous mountain in Wales on account of the frequent bogs, which hold out no warning, concealed as they are under a smooth and apparently firm turf. It should never be attempted without a guide, whose attendance is very precarious. There is however a hovel near the base, which will occasionally furnish a conductor. The leading circumstance in the character of this mountain, is its furnishing a head to the three rivers, all celebrated among both poets and topographers, of Severn, Wye and Rydall.''

H.B. Malkin 1804.

Plynlimon (Pumlumon Fawr).
On the great mass of Plynlimon are the sources of the rivers Severn, Wye and Rheidol. These three rivers, which are known as the three sisters agreed to make a visit to the sea one morning. Severn rose early, and took a route through Shropshire, Worcestershire and Gloucestershire. Wye rose later and took her journey through the counties of Radnorshire and Herefordshire, falling in with her sister near Chepstow and going hand in hand to the sea. (N.B. this was before the days of local Government reorganisation!) Rheidol indulged in her dreams and slept so late that she was forced to take the nearest route to the sea at Aberystwyth.

Water, water everywhere.
It was on the summit of this mountain that the poet Coleridge thought of his famous lines 'water, water everywhere and not a drop to drink.' From the waterless summit he could see all around him various mountain pools and rivulets, and below, many miles to the west, the broad expanse of Cardigan Bay.

Just follow the poles.
''Plynlimon is all but pathless. When the ascent is made from the southern ('Steddfa Gurig) side, there is nothing in the appearance of the mountain to show the direction of the summit, which indeed is not seen until we are close upon it. Some good Samaritan has, however set up a series of guide-posts by following which the climber is able not only to find his way, but to evade the marshes that lie in wait for him if he presumes upon any deflection from the humble course 'from pole to pole'.''

'Gossiping Guide to Wales'. 1904.

Coleridge was wrong!
George Borrow once walked up Plynlimmon from Eisteddfa Gurig Farm on his famous journey through Wild Wales. He visited the summit and drank from the springs of the Wye and the Severn on the upper slopes.

Catch a caterpillar.
''At one time a caterpillar tractor used to ferry tourists from Eisteddfa Gurig farm during the summer holiday period. The trip took one hour and the tractor sometimes made six journeys in one day.''

W.T. Palmer 'The Splendour of Wales'. 1932.

An amusing notice used to be seen at Steddfa Gurig (then an inn), 2½ miles south of the summit, and 13¼ miles by road from Llanidloes: The notorios hill Plinlimon is on these premises: This place, being 1,358′ above the sea, is the best starting point for the ascent of the mountain, and coaches run past it from Llanidloes.''

W.P. Haskett Smith. 'Climbing in the British Isles'. Vol. II 1895.

The Welsh Cinderella.
"Yet further north is the sodden wilderness of Plynlimmon, the high tableland of bog and shale with a summit which is ill-defined and always tantalising elusive and the watersheds of numerous streams. In its plover-haunted recesses, five rivers have their mystic sources, the Severn, Wye, Rheidol. Llyfnant and Clywedog.

Though it has neither the character nor appeal of Snowdon, Cader Idris or the Carmarthen Van there are those who are sensitive to its charms, and it is perhaps the Cinderella of all our mountains."

Tudor Edwards. 'The Face of Wales'. 1950.

Elenith Mountains — wildest Wales.
"It is an empty land of green, tumbled hills and winding streams, with heathery moorland, rocky outcrops on bogs, of some 300 square miles, a dissected plateau of Silurian grits and shales, ranging in height from about 1,000 feet in the river clefts up to some 1,700 on the hills, with one or two little pieces over the 2,000 feet level as at Drygarn Fawr, north of Abergwesyn, a fine viewpoint. It seems nameless, but Giraldus refers to it as 'Elenith,' a term it is now sought to revive."

Tudor Edwards. 'The Face of Wales' 1950.

The heat of the moment.
I sat dripping in front of a blazing fire, having just descended from the Elenith mountains. Sipping my ale I sat with the steam rising from my damp clothes.

The landlord entered the room, presumably to check on the fire and the welfare of his only customer. Wishing to be polite, I said, 'This is one of the best fires that I have seen for a long time.' The man glanced at the fire, grunted and left the room. Two minutes later he returned with a large shovel, stuck it into the fire and carried a pile of blazing coals from the room. He made two journeys and I watched dumbfounded. He left me with one small lump of coal that flickered for a few seconds and then went out. With a shiver I reached for my anorak and I silently vowed that I would never try to make polite conversation in a pub again.
Chris Barber 1972.

The old drovers' road from Abergwesyn to Tregaron passes through the wild and remote Irfon valley. A.G. Bradley once described it as follows. "Road and river, a ribbon of yellow and a twisting thread of silver wander side by side into a land of mystery."

"If the cyclist is callous as to his tyres and is prepared to walk half the way, there is really no reason why he should not follow the old drovers' road on its striking journey to Tregaron and the low country of Cardigan. A sprinkling of farmers in the head of the mountains have no other exit, and though the saddle, to be sure, is their chief means of progress, stout gigs, and carts have frequently to negotiate it, and it is kept in sufficient repair for such rough purposes."

A.G. Bradley 'Highways and Byways in South Wales'. 1903.

The broad expanse of the Claerwen Reservoir in the heart of the Elenith.

The coming of the great waters.

". . .the mountains of Cwm Dauddwr and of Drygarn and Pen y Gorllwyn look down upon these miles of lakes and share their ancient solitudes with the silence of unmolested waters, may you and I, dear reader, be alive to come again and behold a spectacle upon whose possibilities I dare not venture to enlarge."

A.G. Bradley 'Highways and Byways in South Wales'. 1903.

"This will be the largest of all the Welsh dams, some 180 feet high i.e. 60 feet higher than any of the others and the enclosed lake will be about four miles long and nearly twenty miles in circumference with a holding capacity of over 10,000,000,000 gallons.

I am glad to have seen this valley before the great reservoir comes into being, for it is grand country, but not likely to be spoilt, for the engineers of Birmingham are artists at their jobs."

Sid Wright 'Up the Claerwen'. 1948.

One of the massive cairns on the summit of Drygarn Fawr.

Drygarn Fawr with its Christmas pudding cairn.

"After two-and-a-half hours' walking, climbing, stumbling and squelching, we saw our objective before us looming like a round dome on the top of the mountain. We had now reached the summit, and what a panorama to be sure. John with his binoculars could see the sea and Bardsey Island way out in Cardigan Bay. To the north was Snowdon and the nearer heights of Plynlimon. To the south were the long ranges of mountains from Prescelly to the Black Mountains. It is really one of the finest viewpoints I know. Immediately before us to the south was the Irfon Valley and we could pick out Builth Wells some dozen miles away to the south-east. Then I had a closer look at the cairn; it was like a big Christmas pudding in shape, and on the top the white sauce poured over, in the form of a crest of white spar rocks. It is about 25 yards in circumference, thus it is about 25 feet in diameter, and John estimated it at about 15 feet in height. It is symmetrically built and has a mark stone on the top marked B.C. I am afraid that it is not as old as all that, for methinks the letters just mean Birmingham Corporation, since here, at the crest of the mountain, is the limit of their catchment area.

The Ordnance Survey Office first used a cairn on Drygarn Fawr as a Trignometrical Survey Station in 1851 and it must have been the original cairn which had been built hundreds of years before for a vantage point for signalling during the wars Wales fought against England in this area. The extensive view over the whole of Mid-Wales would make it an ideal spot for this purpose. The cairn was rebuilt in 1884 to commemorate the original one, but was not again used by the Ordnance Survey as, for the Retriangulation Survey of Great Britain in 1936 a new station in the form of a concrete pillar was erected some fifty yards from the cairn.''

Sid Wright 'Up the Claerwen'. 1948.

Radnor Forest.
''To discover all the beauties of Radnor Forest one must travel on foot, for much is hidden away behind the hills; but a tour round the forest will finish a succession of splendid views, and perhaps, entice the motorist to make a closer acquaintance with the secrets of the forest. It has four heights over 2,000 ft., viz., Great Rhos 2,166 ft., Black Mixon, 2,135 ft., Great Creigiau, 2,100 ft., and Bach Hill, 2,002 ft., the three former all near the centre of the forest, and many lesser heights, mountain streams innumerable, a celebrated waterfall and many tumuli.''

E.P. Permon. 'By-Roads in South Wales'. 1933.

On the slopes of Whimble, Radnor Forest is a locality where the population is predominately sheep.

"The mountains of Radnorshire are for the most part low and broad-crowned so that they might be converted to purposes of husbandry, if there was not already a larger proportion of ground in hillage, than the confined knowledge and deficient activity of the natives can turn to a lucrative account.

'Heaps of stones, promiscuously thrown down are very common on the Radnorshire mountains. They are found in various situations and of different dimensions. They are always circular, and generally highest in the middle. Their diameter is frequently from sixty to seventy feet."

H.B. Malkin 1804.

The North Escarpment of the Black Mountains.

Black are the Black Mountains.

"The Black Mountains of the Welsh-English Border are a singularly unspoilt group of long and lofty ridges, separated by valleys of diversified charm, and descending steeply towards the Wye on the northern side, and on the southern side less abruptly towards the Usk.

Anyone who first sees these grass-clad, heather-dappled heights abask in sunlight, or when fleecy clouds merely cast patches of shadow, may well be puzzled by the name — why Black Mountains? The answer is that from the Herefordshire side, except when the sun is pouring its rays on their nearer flank, they actually do look Black, even under snow. In dull weather they stand out as a great dark-hued wedge against the grey of the sky, in all weathers, so soon as the sun is well past the meridian, the eastern ridge looms sombrely, passing from slate-blue monochrome to deeper hues as the daylight wanes, and when there is a fine sunset, appearing theatrically silhouetted in inky tone against the western red. Perhaps it was the Saxons who first bestowed the name: it was almost always from this side that they saw these mountains: few of them crossed the Wye, and fewer still crossed it and returned.''

P.J. Jones 'Welsh Border Country' 1938.

Mynydd Pen y Fal otherwise known as the Sugar Loaf.

"The Sugar Loaf is the most beautiful and striking mountain object in the neighbourhood; and though the scenery viewed from its top is less extensive and varied than that from the summit of its neighbour, the Skyrrid Vawr, it is more generally frequented by the inhabitants of Abergavenny in their pleasure excursions.

The view from the Pen-y-Fal is so vast and extensive, that it is impossible to attempt a description of it, beyond saying that northwards appear the magnificent range of the Black Mountains; westwards is seen the Blorenge; directly south, the Bristol Channel; and eastwards a beautiful champaign country, rich with green fields and gentle uplands. The mountain, when viewed from different points, presents a variety of appearances. It looks like a sharp ridge from the opposite side of the Usk, and from a south-easterly direction, it presents to the eye almost a pyramid.''

John White. 'Guide to the Town and Neighbourhood of Abergavenny'. 1877.

Ysgrryd Fawr (Skirrid Fawr) from the north east.

Stricken on the Skirrid In 1797.

"After taking some refreshments and repose, I departed at two for the summit of the Skyrrid, on horseback, and accompanied by the same guide who had conducted me to the top of the Sugar Loaf. Having rode two miles along the road leading to White Castle, we attempted to ascend towards the south-western part of the mountain, which is distinguished with three small fissures. I soon discovered that the guide was unaquainted with the way, and enquiring of a farmer, was informed that the usual route led by Llandewi Skyrrid; by his direction, however, we continued at the foot of the mountain, through fields of corn and pasture, and then proceeded along a narrow path, overspread with high broom, which in many places quite covered my horse. Forcing our way with some difficulty through this heathy wood, we rode over a moor, by the side of the stone wall and hedge which stretch at the base, reached the path leading from Llandewi Skyrrid and ascended, on foot, the grassy slope of the mountain.

The heat was so intense, the fatigue I had undertaken in the day so considerable, and the effort I impatiently made to reach the summit so violent, that when I looked down from the narrow and desolated ridge, the boundless expanse around and beneath, which suddenly burst upon my sight, overcame me. I felt a mixed sensation of animation and lassitude, horror and delight, such as I scarcely ever before experienced even in the Alps of Switzerland; my spirits almost failed, even curiosity was suspended, and I threw myself exhausted on the ground. These sensations increased during my continuance on the summit: I several times attempted to walk along the ridge, but my head became so giddy as I looked down the precipitous sides, and particularly towards the great fissure, that I could not remain standing.

I seemed only safe when extended on the ground, and was not therefore in a condition to examine and describe the beauties of the view. However, I took out my pencil, and made a few hasty notes. The ridge of the Skyrrid seemed to be about a mile in length, extremely narrow, in general not more than thirty or forty feet broad, and in some places only ten or twelve; its craggy surface is partly covered with scant and russet herbage, and exhibits only a stunted thorn, which heightens the dreariness of its aspect. After remaining half an hour on the top, incapable of making any further observations, I descended, and went round the eastern side of the mountain, where it terminates in an abrupt precipice near the large fissure."

Archdeacon William Coxe 'Historial Tour through Monmouthshire' 1801.

"On fair clear days one could see the pointed summit of the Holy Mountain by Abergavenny. It would shine, I remember, a pure blue in the far sunshine; it was a mountain peak in a fairy tale."

Arthur Machen. 'Far off things.'

"Cloud shadows on the Sugar Loaf, the song a river sings
When touched by rain's soft finger tips, those sudden, mellow gleams
Of sunlight on old Skirrid — these are the magic things
That I have stored within my heart and woved into dreams . . ."

Myfanwy Haycock.

The Brecon Beacons

The magnificent skyline of the high summits of the Brecon Beacons from Pen y Crug camp near Brecon.

More horrid and frightful than the Alps.

Entering Powys from the north Daniel Defoe on his tour of Great Britain in 1724-6 found the mountains of Breconshire in some places more "horrid and frightful than the Alps." *He complained,* "we were saluted with Mounch-denny Hill (Pen-y-Fan) on our left, and the Black Mountain on the right, and all a ridge of horrid rocks and precipices between, over which, if we had not had a trusty guide, we should never have found our way; and indeed we began to repent our curiosity, as not met with anything worth the trouble; and a country looking so full of horror, that we thought to have given over the enterprise, and have left Wales out of our circuit."

The ascent of Pen-y-Fan from Storey Arms in 1903.

"At an elevation of nearly 1400 feet a lonely inn known as the Storey Arms looks down over a wild country towards Glamorganshire. *The existing building bears the same name, but is no longer an inn and does not stand on quite the same site).*

It is not an attractive looking tavern, and is given over I should imagine, more to the thirsty son of toil on his way to the murky regions of Merthyr and the south than to the mountaineer, but is perhaps sufficient for the occasion.

The ascent from this side is a long up hill drag rather than a climb. The peak of Pen-y-Fan is about 1600 feet above the inn and out of sight in any weather. There is no beaten track and the route is quite vague."

Note

Today this same path is hardly vague for it is now often referred to as the 'Tourist Track' or the MI.

"When I had groped my way, up over the rough moor grasses and spongy bogs to the foot of the crags that crown the summit of Corn du, and scrambled up them, the horizontal had contracted to a radius of five to twenty yards, though the wind was blowing at such a rate I was glad enough to find shelter in the crannies of the rocks. That further progress would have been rash without a knowledge of the ground I was well aware, from some familiarity with the shape of the mountains as seen from below, and purposeless in any case. Reward came, however, on this occasion sooner than looked for. For perhaps half an hour I had contemplated the endless rush of floating vapour, sometimes tantalising one with a momentary glimpse of green below, and then again mixing with the very smoke of one's pipe. A hawk dashed by anon and now and again a crow sailing up with the wind into the mist over the precipice that I rightly conjectured lay ahead of us. A rock ousel, bred no doubt in these same crags blundered into my immediate presence to the astonishment and terror of that shy hunter of wild places, but a wheatear, having surveyed me calmly and critically, proved sociable, and chirped around as if the occasion was quite a cheerful and conventional one. Gradually the clouds lightened and lifted: the peak of Pen-y-Fan, or Arthur's Chair, showed but a few hundred yards off and two or three hundred feet higher, and I lost no time in getting to the top of the hughest point in South Wales."

A.G. Bradley 'Highways and byways in South Wales' 1903.

The power of the wind.

The Geographer Speed once ascended to the top of Pen-y-Fan, the highest mountain in South Wales (2,906') and later wrote:—

". . . were it not that I have witnessess to affirm what I say, I should blush to let the report thereof pass from my pen. From the top of that hill called Mounch Denny, or Cader Arthur, they had oftentimes cast from them, and down the north east side, their cloaks, hats and staves, which not withstanding would never fall, but were there with the air and wind still returned back and blown up, neither said they, will anything descend from that cliff, being so cast, unless it be stones or some metallic substance; affirming the cause to be clouds which are seen to racke much lower than the mountain."

Above the clouds looking towards Pen y Fan and Corn Du in the Brecon Beacons.

"The Beacons reach high in heaven in
Pen-y-Fan, and Corn Ddu, the indigo
Corniced throne of an intriguing moorland."

Tudor Edwards. 'The Face of Wales'. 1950.

A man falls 12,000′ !??

". . . Sandstone peaks of very striking outline. Indeed, 'Mackintosh (who saw them from the east) says, 'I was more impressed than I have ever been with any mountain in Wales. Their outline executed a very unusual idea of sublimity!'

A curious notion once prevailed that nothing would fall from the top of this hill. Many years ago an unfortunate picknicker disproved this. See the Times Index but the statement there made that he fell 12,000′ is somewhat startling."

W.P. Haskett Smith. 'Climbing in the British Isles'. Vol. II 1895.

The highest car park in South Wales.

Some years ago I carried a parking meter down from the snow covered summit of Pen-y-Fan, which at 2,906′ is the highest mountain in South Wales.

This unlikely piece of equipment had been stolen in London by students during rag week and transported nearly 200 miles to the Brecon Beacons. As I brought it down the mountainside, the meter rattled with money and seemed to feel progressively heavier. Eventually I reached Brecon and walked into the police station.

A poker faced policeman, behind the reception desk yawned and asked me, 'What have you got there?' Feeling stupid I replied, 'A parking meter.' 'Where did you get it?' he returned, as if this were an every day occurrence. 'I found it on top of Pen-y-Fan.' I said. The policeman did not even blink. 'Oh, in the Beacons, just a minute and I'll write out a receipt for it.'

I still have the receipt. The wording told me that if the object was not claimed within 14 days then I could keep it. Needless to say, I did not return to the police station, but sometimes I wonder if I am in fact the legal owner of a parking meter?

Chris Barber 1967.

The north east face of Pen y Fan from Cwm Sere.

Doorstep Climbing.
"Here right on my doorstep, so to speak, I found one of the most severe and technically difficult climbs I have ever attempted, anywhere during some 30 years of climbing!! I allude to the magnificent north-east face of Pen-y-Fan in the Brecon Beacons. The conquest of this face, taken straight up and over the upper rampart of vertical rock at the summit, will yield climbing of a severity fully up to anything encountered in Wales. If anyone reading this is inclined to scoff, let him make the ascent under severe winter conditions and he will fully endorse what I have written. There are patches on this face which, with snow and ice on the mountain, will tax the expert to his very limits."

R.G. Sandeman. 'A Mountaineer's Journal'. 1949

The Direct Route up the North East Face.
"Pen y Fan now fairly got into our blood. The preliminary climbs had thoroughly aroused our determination to make the direct climb up the great north east face from base to summit.

My preliminary investigations had convinced me that the thing was quite within the bounds of the justifiable for experienced mountaineers. But it would obviously involve climbing of an extremely severe and delicate nature. And it would also be dangerous.

A mountain may be very difficult but not dangerous . . . but the north east face of Pen y Fan is both difficult and dangerous as well.

Luckily both Davies and myself knew exactly the limits of each other's powers. Each had perfect confidence in the other, and that is one of the secrets of successful and safe climbing. Had my companion been untried, or had I not the most intimate knowledge of his powers as a climber, I would never have attempted this ascent with him.

Accordingly, one winter morning, we arrived at the foot of the great precipice just as the mists were lifting from the hills.

Winter had gripped the mountains for some weeks. An iron frost bound the land. We had trudged up the wild valley through some six inches of snow and a dense mist. Then, as we arrived at the foot of our climb, the clouds began to lift, breaking in great masses of swirling grey vapour, and rising slowly upwards under the sun rays. Soon the entire mountain was clear of the mists and we gazed upwards at a scene of really awe-inspiring grandeur. Seen from the base, the north east face of Pen y Fan, in such winter conditions as prevailed that morning, looks every inch like an Alpine peak. Even in summer time it looks savage and forbidding, but to-day, in its snowy covering, it appeared quite terrific. There was scarcely a spot of black to be seen on the whole great precipice. Huge icicles hung from every ledge and buttress of rock. The almost vertical grass slopes between the rock walls which run along the entire face, were deep in snow.

Delicate drifts had formed along the steep slopes and were moulded by the winds into weird curves and lines. And high above, outlined against the blue winter skies, the great summit rampart of vertical cliffs which guard the top, looked the very embodiment of grim inaccessibility.

Let those who declare that South Wales possesses no real climbing, gaze at this place under such conditions, and they will quickly change their opinion.

We stood there for some time and examined every foot of the huge face.

"Well . . ."? exclaimed Davies . . . "what about it?"

I confess that I did not know what to think.

R.G. Sandeman wearing his special windproof suit which he no doubt used on the first ascent of the Central Gulley of Pen y Fan, with Alfred Davies in 1939.

"We will just see how it goes . . ." I answered.

Davies did not reply. He looked miserably at me and shook his head.

We roped up. We had 60 feet of rope between us. I advanced to the assault. My nerves were tingling with that thrill of intense excitement every climber knows. As far as I knew no one had made this direct ascent before. Parties had tried and had been forced back.

I had read some years before that a party from Oxford or Cambridge . . . I forget which had declared the difficulties encountered to be as technically severe as those of the ordinary route up the Matterhorn. . . a statement which is probably incorrect.

An easy scramble up the snow covered boulders and debris brought me to the foot of the climb proper. This consists of a very steep grass slope set at a high angle and with a line of vertical rock some fifty feet up the slope. Snow to the depth of some six inches covered everything. To the right are vertical and overhanging rocks which bound the great central gully. These rocks are impossible, and thus one has to keep well away to their left. An awkward bit of scrambling brought me below the first outcrop of rocks which run in a series of vertical walls all along the face between the grass slopes. In fact, the whole difficulty of the north east face of Pen y Fan consists of surmounting a series of exceedingly steep grass slopes, and vertical walls of rock, and very steep and treacherous slopes of crumbling red shale. There are places where one has to mount upon the second man's shoulder, and then, at arms length, get a grip upon the very doubtful holds, while one's companion gives a push with his ice axe to one's feet to enable one to get over the top of the rock barriers. This method of progress is well enough when done on sound rock . . . but when the second man is standing in very doubtful footholds in an almost vertical grass slope, and this same slope is covered with six inches of powdery snow, the sensations of the unfortunate leader are apt to be a trifle too vivid. For a slip on the part of either leader or second man when engaged in these delicate operations, is likely to be followed by the direct results. When, in addition to deep snow, the rocks are glazed with ice, and huge icicles hang from every ledge and rock, and a biting east wind is blowing, it will be soon borne in upon the climber's consciousness that this ascent is for experts only.

We slowly gained height. Nowhere was it possible to move two at a time. Had the snow frozen like the Scottish snow, these steep grass slopes would have been delightful to cut one's way up . . . but with the snow soft and powdery they were simply devilish. It was almost impossible to make a safe foothold. And the bitter east wind was numbing one's fingers till all feeling began to fail. Some two hundred feet up the face I began to realise that this place was one of the most dangerous and difficult I had ever attempted. A glance downwards proved the absolute certainty of disaster should a slip occur.

Up and up we toiled, foot by foot. Then we came to a vertical grass slope topped by a wall of rock which overhung slightly. It was sheeted in a frozen mail of ice. To storm this took the most desperate struggle which I have, I think, ever been called upon to make. Standing on Davies's shoulders I got a grip at full arms length upon the frozen turf along the top of the barrier. But I could only reach it with my finger tips and Davies had to give me a push with his ice axe to enable me to at last draw myself up till I was lying gasping on the edge of the top. In this precarious position I found that there was no hold by which I could drag myself up to the almost vertical slope above. My half frozen fingers scraped and dug into the snow, but nothing in the way of a hold could be found.

And I was slowly slipping backwards. By an effort which left me almost dead beat. I somewhat riggled upwards with the point of my axe droven into the frozen turf above. Below me, Davies had luckily been unaware of the critical situation in which his leader had been placed for those few breathless moments. Having rested a few minutes I made myself as secure as the almost total absence of anything to secure myself to would admit, and then helped Davies up over the forbidding wall of rock. As he had no one upon whose shoulder he could stand to reach the tip of the rock, I had to haul his dead weight bodily upwards for some six feet before he could reach a hold at all.

And anyone who has seen Alfred Davies will readily admit that to haul him up for even six feet is no mean feat . . . for he is no feather weight! The severity of this particular pitch can be realised when I state that even for the second man, with all the aid of the rope, it is by no means an easy bit of scrambling. I imagine that there must be other ways past this place by a traverse either to left or right, and if there are it would be advisable for future parties to find them! Above this sinister spot the snow covered grass slope was practically vertical, and above this was another rock wall of most forbidding appearance. And, of course, everything was a mass of snow and the shale and turf below it like iron from the intense frost. If there is anything . . . in the whole of Wales . . . to match this spot for danger and difficulty of an extremely sinister type, then I have yet to see it. Were this place composed of good, firm rock, then it would be classed as a difficult but pleasant climb . . . but composed as it is of almost vertical grass and treacherous shale with a perpendicular wall of rotten red sandstone at the top, it is simply devilish.

A short ice pitch in Right Hand Gully — North East Face of Pen y Fan.

And just as we were struggling with its difficulties, down came the mists in a dense blanket of swirling vapour! Things really looked serious. Only once before have I been in such a situation . . and then on good sound rock, with the way clear before me, for I knew the route.

The storming of this slope and the ascent of the rock wall called for every bit of skill and climbing craft of which I was capable. How we ever got up at all is somewhat of a mystery.

With frozen fingers gripping frozen rocks and turf we slowly gained height. Every single foothold had to be dug out of the shale, turf, and soil, and none of these even approached what may be called safe . . . Then at the top of the grass slope came the rock wall . . . absolutely vertical and even slightly overhanging at the top.

The mists and falling snow were so dense that one could only see some twenty feet ahead at times. Luckily the wind had fallen to a dead calm. A short traverse to the right brought me to a spot from which the rock wall yielded after a short but desperate struggle. It again became necessary to mount my companion's shoulders before a hold could be gained. This hold proved to be a finger grip on a frozen stone embedded in the soil at the top of the rock. It was snow covered and as cold as charity.

Helped by a shove from the ice axe under my feet from Davies, I found myself lying panting and breathless in the snow on a slope which was so steep that it was difficult to prevent slipping back.

After resting for a few moments I managed to make a tolerable anchorage with my ice axe and then got Davies up to me.

Above this spot the slope went on into the mists at an alarming angle. Up this we fought our way foot by foot. Then another rock wall. Then more steep slope and we were brought up by a veritable Styx, in the form of a wall down which an enormous mass of ice had formed by the running water down the place. This great crust of ice was about a foot thick and had the form of a great wrinkled white wall. Never in Wales have I seen such a truly arctic looking scene. However, as often happens in mountaineering, the place was not so difficult as it appeared at first. I cut out some steps in the ice while standing on Davies's shoulders and after a tough struggle stormed this sinister looking spot.

Good sound footing was obtained above from which I hauled my companion up like a sack of flour. Then on we went again, over rocks and grass slopes and treacherous shale covered by powdery snow. We guessed that by now we must be nearing the final problem of the summit rampart of the rocks. These, we judged would be of extreme difficulty, and we were so used to difficulties by now that we regarded them as mere stepping stones to the summit of Pen y Fan.

Another wall of rock landed up upon the great shale slope which we knew lay immediately below the final escarpment the summit barrier of rocks. This shale slope was some six inches deep in that abominable powdery snow, and the shale beneath it was frozen like iron. It is not very steep, but steep enough to make a slip deadly dangerous in the conditions then existing. And it was extremely difficult NOT to slip. The steps one cut in the frozen shale were terribly rotten and insecure. Then, at the top of this slope we found ourselves at last beneath the summit cliffs.

Through the mists and falling snow they loomed up like great white and grey walls. To the right they were obviously utterly impossible. But directly above us were a series of good ledges which, although plastered with snow and ice, looked just within the bounds of practical climbing. We went at them with grim determination. More shoulder work ensued before I gained the first ledge. Here it was just possible to stand and help my companion up to me. Then a nasty traverse enabled me to gain another sloping ledge. The next part of the proceedings will enable the man who thinks there is no real climbing in South Wales, to alter his opinions. One has to swing by one's finger tips and then haul oneself up till one's chest rests upon a sloping, turf covered ledge before any safe hold can be gained. This turf ledge was some inches deep in remarkable cold snow. To gain an upright attitude on this ledge calls for a considerable skill in the art of balance.

The severity of the situation made poor Davies call out in agonised tones . . "For God's sake . . . don't slip . . . I can't hold you here."

If you knew Alfred Davies you would appreciate the rather critical situation which called forth these words. I have never known him to say such a thing before or since.

From that point on the climbing becomes less severe. At last we drew ourselves over the last pitch and stood upon the snowy summit . . . triumphant but a trifle breathless and trembling.

The North East face of Pen y Fan with a light covering of snow but providing a good view of the Central Gulley.

Davies let out one of his yells . . . which can be heard at least a mile away! We sat down in the snow and eat our lunch.

So ended the conquest of the north east face of Pen y Fan.

The ascent is one of extreme difficulty . . . but it was made doubly so by the wintery conditions under which we did it. Needless to state this climb should be left severely alone except by experienced climbers. I cannot stress this too strongly. Should some party of foolish young and inexperienced climbers read of this ascent and attempt it, disaster is almost sure to happen.

Therefore, I cannot too strongly stress that everyone, save those possessing the ability and experience to overcome the very severe technical difficulties involved in this climb, should leave it alone.

And if, in spite of this warning, a fatal accident occurs on this dangerous spot, then, at least, I shall not feel to blame.

But there are a variety of scrambles on Pen y Fan which anyone possessing some little experience of climbing can easily tackle.

The great central gully is easy enough, and the big gullies to the extreme right afford easy scrambles. Owing to the outbreak of the war in 1939 we were unable to work out the numerous other routes which undoubtedly exist on this fine face. An expert party could find many climbs here, ranging from easy work to the most severe ascents. We shall return when the present hostilities cease and the petrol is again available!

But as I end this book the war has reached its full fury, a rain of death is falling upon London from the skies—and the ''High Tops'' seem very far away!''

R.G. Sandeman. 'A Mountaineer's Journal'. 1949.

Bannau Brycheiniog in the Carmarthen Fans.

"Fan Frynach and Fan Giherich, Fan Brycheiniog and Fan-hir, rolling away one behind the other, a confusion of dark and rugged masses into Carmarthenshire (though none of them three thousand feet in altitude), made as savage and striking a picture as one could wish for."

A.G. Bradley 'Highways and byways in South Wales' 1903.

The yellow green grass of Wales.
". . . these lower slopes of the Welsh hills are covered with grass of a peculiar greenish-yellow tint, and it does not vary much at any time of year. Those of us who know it well would not exchange it for the June flowers of the Tyrol, nor the tropical luxuriance of the Conca d'Oro. Its homely beauty and perfect fitness reminds us of some simple garment worn by one whom we loved when we were young. Many artists have tried to paint these Welsh mountain slopes — but few can be said to have succeeded in capturing the elusive charms of the close yellow-green grass."

Charles Kingsley. (He visited Wales in the 1850's.)

Land of the Leek
"Give me the grey hilltops where storm winds are wild,
And the mountains and rocks that I climbed as a child.
Give me the brave streams that rush down to the shore,
To greet the great waves that come in with a roar,
Where'er I may go and wherever I seek,
I'll ne'er find a land like the Land of the Leek".

Trefin

Meditations on Welsh mountains.

Above Llyn y Fan fach — Carmarthen Fans.

The true mountaineer.
"He is one who not only enjoys climbing mountains, but is never so happy as when he is among mountains and is able to see, smell and hear mountains. He has what Mr. Geoffrey Winthrop Young terms a 'feeling' for mountains. Mountains are not things to be seen and climbed for a week or so every year; they are always present somewhere at the back of the mind, ready to spring into the forefront at all times and in all manner of places."

F.S. Smythe. 'The Mountain Vision' 1941.

"Mountaineering can never be learned from books. The only way to become a mountaineer is through long and most assiduous practice on the mountains themselves. The art of climbing within limits, may be learned by most persons who have the urge and the love of the High Tops, and who are patient enough to proceed by slow degrees."

R.G. Sandeman. 'A Mountaineer's Journal'. 1949.

Hard men.
"There is no more obnoxious person than the man who sets out to be a 'he man'. For such there should be a special mountain or jungle set apart where they may devour unpalatable ill-cooked food tasting of paraffin to their heart's content, sleep on the knobbly stones, shiver in insufficient clothing, and remain unshaven and unwashed."

"For a syborite like myself, comfort is always preferable to discomfort. I do not enjoy getting wet and grubby; I dislike a chilly bivouac, numbed fingers on a climb an anathema; the poor food, worse cooking and perpetual taste of paraffin regarded by some as synonymous with Himalayan mountaineering seem to me to be unnecessary and undesirable. I climb to enjoy myself and the scenery, not to pose as an atavistic 'he man'."

F.S. Smythe. 'The Mountain Vision'. 1941.

Boots V Alpenstocks.
"My father tells me that he once climbed to the Fox's path and near the top of the steep part he met a party coming down. They were curiously equipped with tennis shoes and alpenstocks. He went on to the top of the mountain, stayed there a few minutes, descended without hurrying himself, and passed the same party before they had reached the bottom of the scree. The moral is that if boots are worn an alpenstock will not be required."

Patrick Monkhouse. 'On Foot in North Wales'. 1934.

Mountaineers love dark brown maps.
"A map is a good thing. A map of North Wales is a very good thing. So much of it is dark brown, some is even purple, and that is higher than brown. If one dwells in the lowlands it is a deal of comfort to eye-travel the dark brown occasionally and to remember."

A.M. Eastwood. 'A Day on Welsh Hills.'

"Maps are always a treasured possession of the mountaineer. They are the charts by which he steers his course, they enable him to plan his journeys beforehand, guide him in carrying out those plans, and above all, perhaps, they serve to recall his memories of great days spent amongst the hills. Maps are essential to a full enjoyment of his sport and under some conditions may be essential to his safety."

G.A. Lister 1924.

Welsh distance.
". . . In the heart of Wild Wales it is always better to measure distance in terms of time as they do in Switzerland. What is the use of being told that the distance, say from Lauterbrunnen to Wengen is two miles? Far more satisfactory is it to know that in order to reach that delectable Alpine village you have to struggle and pant for two hours. And so when we say that the distance between Glyn Ceiriog and Llangollen is three miles it should be added in common fairness that those miles consists of a terribly steep climb up one side of the ridge, a few yards of comparatively level road on the top, and a most precipitous descent on the other side. But no person who dislikes stiff climbs has any business to be in Wales at all: for him the Leamingtons and the Cheltenhams of the world have been created, and he had better stick to them! Anyone of ordinary soundness of limb and wind would enjoy this climb over the Berwyns, with its exhilarating air and its extensive prospects."

W. Watkin Davies. 'A Wayfarer in Wales'. 1930.

Have I got time? — The Sugar Loaf.

A question of scale — hills or mountains?

"In those parts of Wales where there are no real mountains and the highest local hill is made a pet of, and given mountain status. Thus in Anglesey they are not content with the vision of Snowdon and his brethren at a distance but they must have their own. So they have given the described title and status to Holyhead Mountain (720 feet) . . . while the good people of Flint sport a mountain 250 feet high. It is not that they lack the proper word, either, for if these summits had had real mountains adjacent to them they would have been called 'bryn and not 'mynydd'."

Edmund Vale. 'The World of Wales'. 1935.

Two proverbs.

"Hills are for the happy-go-lucky rambler who likes to sing as he goes. Mountains are made of sterner stuff: they demand the climbers' undivided attention.'

'On a hill you can afford to be cocksure, on a mountain never'."

W.K. Richmond. 'Climbers Testament'. 1950.

Hills can be horrific!

"When all is said and done, mere size is no criterion. In the Radnor Forest there is a modest eminence called Whimble which falls short of the 2,000 feet mark — yet after a Christmas snowstorm it might easily pass for another Cairn Toul. Moel Hebog is neither more nor less than a burly hill, but see it loom above Beddgelert in the darkness of a thunder shower and you will agree that it has its horrific aspects."

W.K. Richmond. 'Climbers Testament'. 1950.

"We see in mountains what we take to them. The big things of this Earth need a certain bigness of mind and spirit in the beholder for their due appreciation. We may see in these mountains either mere masses of barren rocks . . . or we may realise that they are not only the 'causes of circulation of water on the earth, and so the sources of our physical well-being, but they are also places where we may escape from the plain and humdrum life, where we may rise above ourselves, and, in more than one crowded hour of glorious life, have bodily experiences, as well as intellectual insight and spiritual perceptions of things unseen, that shall serve for true re-creation of body and soul."

Valentine Davies. 'A Guide to Snowdon' 1936.

Rain — one of Wales's greatest assets.
"Over the whole of Wales, in the year 1913, the rain fall was 44.3 inches, while for the whole of England it was only 27.8 inches. Yet the number of days on which rain fell in Wales was 205, and England 182. The rain showers in Wales must therefore be heavier than in England."

R. Owen/J.E. Roberts. 'The Story of Montgomeryshire'. 1916.

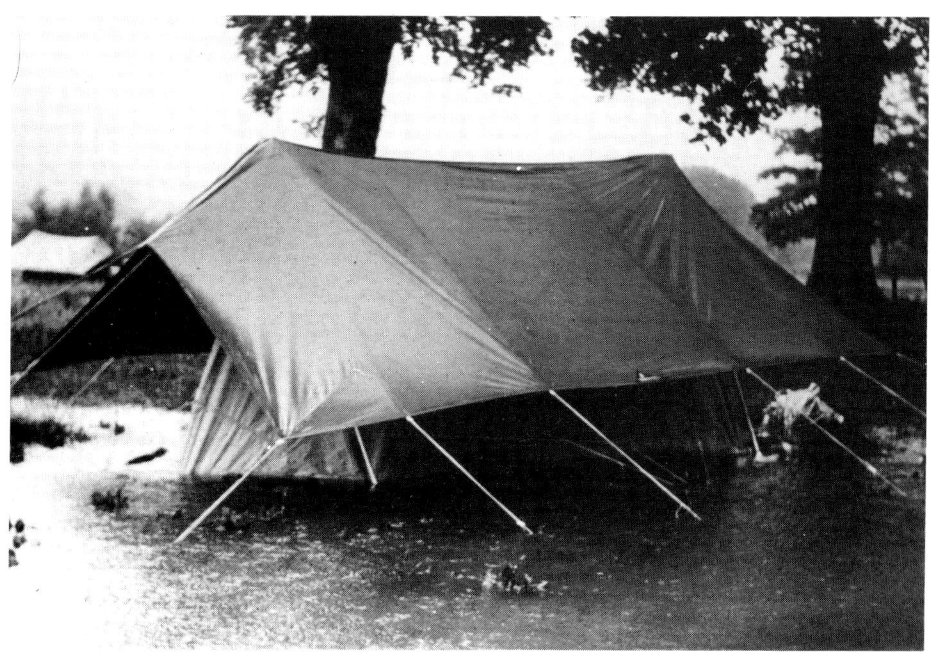

The result of three days of incessant Snowdonia rain.

Yes it still pours with rain in Wales — just as hard as ever before. One night after three days of torrential rain I lay snugly on my airbed, reading a book, when I suddenly came to the conclusion that I was floating. The sewn in ground sheet of my tent was endeavouring to keep out the rising water, until I foolishly put my hand on it and pushed downwards. To my horror the water came bubbling through the floor of the tent. Fortunately, I had a large polythene survival bag with me and I had the presence of mind to grab it and quickly stuff my sleeping bag inside it. Remaining on the airbed I managed to stay inside the tent and had a reasonable nights sleep — waking in the morning to find that the bottom end of the tent and my polythene outer shell in six inches of water.

Chris Barber 1975.

Truly delectable situations.
"The cliffs, the oblique rain across the slopes of the Carnedds, the purple chaos of rocks heaped out into a gusty Ogwen, the spongy masses of sphagnum in the swamps, the clean-bitten turf, the drier shelves above, the endless crying of the streams and dark gulf at evening of the lower valley. Mornings when Y Garn and Foel Goch soar up into the shrouds of lifting cloud and the lake glitters through the curtain of the rowans with their dark coral berries. The springiness of the bilberry clumps as you lie in the sunshine on the Heather Terrace, the squeak of the lambs as you wind down between the long snouted rocks. Out of all these there is composed a bodily feeling, nameless and definite and irreplaceable like a scent or a taste or an ache. When one is away, some accident — a sheep's baa, a lichen patch on a stone wall — awaken it; but it is none of these things. It is the reverberation of ones life among them, known completely only to those who have lived the same life among the mountains."

Dorothy Pilley. 'Climbing Days' 1935.

Shafts of sunlight.
"The sun-shafts slanting athwart a gully, the blue cloud-shadows that haul themselves over the slopes, the way a pinnacle spins as it launches clear of vapours — these and a thousand others, are the tricks of enchantment."

W.K. Richmond 'Climbers Testament'. 1950.

Looking towards the cliffs of Lliwedd with shafts of evening sunlight cutting across the summit.

Aflowing tide of light.
"Folding like an airy vest,
The very clouds had sunk to rest;
Light gilds the rugged mountain's breast,
Calmly as they lay below;
Every hill seemed topped with snow
As the flowing tide of light
Broke the slumbers of the night."

Ruskin.

"We know the joy of the first smell of the moorland and the first kiss of the mountain wind; and, when the day is ended, as we swing our weary bodies homeward down the valley, we all find an echo in our hearts to the praise of the ancient psalmist, for certainly to us is 'a day in thy courts better than a thousand'."

Herbert Carr. 'The Mountains of Snowdonia'. 1925.

On the Monks' Path in Wildest Wales.

Solitude.

"There are days, when the winds rest and the mists hang sullen and brooding on the hills. Everything is hushed, and earth and sky unite in a sombre monotone. In these mists is silence and a great loneliness. Traverse the hills on such a day and you will know a solitude such as you have never known before. It is not the solitude of a town, nor the solitude of a desert, but a solitude which has in it a message infinitely peaceful, the solitude of the hills."

F.S. Smythe. 'The Mountain Vision'. 1941.

SELECTED BIBLIOGRAPHY

Abraham, George and Ashley. 'Rock Climbing in North Wales' 1906.
Baker E.A. 'The British Highlands with Rope and Rucksack' 1933.
Bagley A.L. 'Holiday Rambles in North Wales' 1925.
Bingley Rev.W. 'Tour round North Wales' 1798.
Borrow, George. 'Wild Wales' 1854.
Carr, H.R.C. and Lister, G.A. 'The Mountains of Snowdonia' 1925.
Cliffe, J.H. 'Notes and recollections of an Angler' 1860.
Coxe, W. 'Historical Tour of Monmouthshire' 1801.
Davies, W. Watkin. 'A Wayfarer in Wales' 1930.
Hutton, W. 'North Wales' 1803.
Jones, P.J. 'Welsh Border Country' 1938.
Monkhouse, P. 'On Foot in North Wales' 1934.
Moore, J. 'Tramping through Wales' 1933.
Morton, H.V. 'In Search of Wales' 1932.
Palmer, W.T. 'The Splendour of Wales' 1932.
Pennant, Thomas. 'A Tour in Wales' 1781.
Pilley, D. 'Climbing Days' 1935.
Richmond, W.K. 'Climber's Testament' 1950.
Roscoe, T. 'Wanderings and Excursions in South Wales' 1939.
Sandeman, R.G. 'A Mountaineer's Journal' 1949.
Smith, W.P. Haskett. 'Climbing in the British Isles Vol II' 1895.
Smythe, F.S. 'The Spirit of the Hills' 1935.
Smythe, F.S. 'The Mountain Vision' 1941.
Smythe, F.S. 'Over Welsh Hills' 1945.
Styles, Showell. 'The Mountaineer's Weekend Book' 1952.
Thomson, J.M. Archer. 'The climbs on Lliwedd' 1909.
Thomson, J.M. Archer. 'Climbing in the Ogwen District' 1910.
White, J. 'Guide to the Town and Neighbourhood of Abergavenny' 1877.
Wright, S. 'Up the Claerwen' 1948.
Young, G.W., Sutton, G. & Noyce W. 'Snowdon Biography' 1957.

ACKNOWLEDGEMENTS

This anthology has taken a number of years to compile and it involved a considerable amount of research. I am particularly grateful to several friends who loaned me copies of relevant books, some of which are much sought after. In particular I would like to thank Paul and Kath Johnson of Llangorse who have one of the finest collections of mountaineering books that I have seen. In addition I would like to thank Bill Barber for his help and encouragement and Michael Blackmore for drawing the map of the Welsh mountains and for his artwork on the cover. My sincere gratitude is also due to Showell Styles for kindly writing the foreword and for allowing me to include his humorous poem 'The Ballad of the Idwal Slabs' which was first published in 'The Mountaineers Weekend Book' by Seeley Service and Co. (London). Also I pass on my thanks to numerous friends in the Gwent Mountaineering Club who over the years have unwittingly posed for many of the photographs that appear on many of the pages of this book.

I thank Methuen and Co. for extracts from A.G. Bradley's 'Highways and Byways in South Wales' and 'A Wayfarer in Wales' by W. Watkin Davies. Also Eyre and Spottiswood and Nea Morin for an extract from 'A Woman's Reach'; and Mrs Sandeman for an extract from 'A Mountaineer's Journal' by R.G. Sandeman, published by Druid Press. The majority of the authors of extracts included in this book are now long passed on and several of the publishers are no longer in existence, but I thank them all for their contribution to the literature of the Welsh mountains.

OTHER TITLES BY CHRIS BARBER

Walks in the Brecon Beacons, Pridgeon 1976 (Out of print).

Exploring the Waterfall Country, Pridgeon 1976. (Out of print).

Ghosts of Wales, John Jones, Cardiff 1979 (Out of print).

Exploring the Brecon Beacons National Park, Regional Publications 1980/85.

Exploring Gwent, Regional Publications 1984.

Mysterious Wales, David and Charles (hardback) 1982, Granada (Paladin Paperback) 1983.

Cordell Country, Blorenge Books 1985.

More Mysterious Wales, David and Charles (hardback) 1986.

Cover picture — back (Chris Barber).
Brecon Beacons summits of Pen-y-Fan and Corn Du from Craig Cerrig-gleisiad.